MODERN BELGIAN LITERATURE

BY THE SAME AUTHOR

An Introduction to the Study of Comparative Education
Power and Politics in Belgian Education
None can be called Deformed
(Problems of the Crippled Adolescent)
Teaching a Modern Language

VERNON MALLINSON

Reader in Education, University of Reading

Modern
Belgian Literature

1830 – 1960

BARNES & NOBLE, Inc.

NEW YORK

PUBLISHERS AND BOOKSELLERS SINCE 1873

Printed in Great Britain

Contents

Preface

In MY preface to an earlier book (*Power and Politics in Belgian Education*) I felt it necessary to record that 'Belgian effort . . . in the field of literature has often been ignored or ungenerously dismissed because of the greater publicity accorded the efforts of other European powers'. It was disturbing to discover how few people knew of the impetus given to the Symbolist movement from Belgium; how so many people assumed that Maeterlinck and Michaux – and even the ubiquitous Simenon – were French; and how little generally was known even of the existence of a number of other writers (both French and Flemish speaking) who have made vital contributions to the main stream and development of modern European literature. Thus I have planned this book with the deliberate intention of filling this gap. The writing of it has given me many pleasurable hours and sent me back to a reading and re-reading of many Belgian authors. If it gives the reader of it the same amount of pleasure and the same urge to familiarize himself with the Belgian literary scene it will more than have justified itself.

Finally, that such a book as this is long overdue will become evident from a quick glance at the select bibliography to be found on page 199. Professor Jethro Bithell is the only English writer to have attempted such a survey and his work was published between 1911 and 1917. Professor Emile Cammaerts (that genial expatriate and exhilarating talker) gave us something of *The Treasure House of Belgium* in 1924. The first full biographical and critical study of Maeterlinck to be published in English was that of my friend and colleague, W. D. Halls. It appeared in 1960.

University of Reading   VERNON MALLINSON
1966

CHAPTER ONE

Nineteenth-Century Renaissance

I

D URING the seventeenth and eighteenth centuries French and Flemish literature of Belgian origin had to all intents and purposes ceased to exist. French culture and the French way of life and thought dominated throughout Belgium. And as the Austrian régime collapsed before the Revolution and the Empire, so did the tendency towards complete cultural identification with France accentuate itself. It was not easily remembered that there had been published as early as the twelfth century an excellent prose translation into Flemish of the psalms; that there had been a strikingly original epic poem about Charlemagne (*Carel ende Elegast*); that a version of Reynart the Fox, which surpassed all others for its masterly animal-epic treatment, and which had been translated into modern German by Goethe, was also Flemish. Similarly, besides travellers' tales innumerable all written in French by Belgian authors, there existed the chronicles of Jean Froissart (?1337–?1410), the memoirs of Philippe de Commynes (?1445–1511), and the dazzling output of the last of the writers of the *ancien régime*, Charles-Joseph de Ligne (1735–1814), who was at one and the same time poet, dramatist, literary critic – and Austrian field-marshal!

It needed, in point of fact, the decision taken by the powers assembled at the Congress of Vienna (1814–15) to combine the Belgian and Dutch Netherlands to form one state, the kingdom of the United Netherlands, both to awaken a Belgian national pride and to stimulate renewed interest in Flemish and Belgian-French culture. It was only natural that Flemish intellectuals and littérateurs should turn their attention to Dutch literature and culture, and it was equally natural that William of Holland should give them every encouragement. Thus, courses in Dutch literature now became available in all universities. A new training college for elementary teachers, opened at Lierre in 1817, gave all its instruction in Dutch and was from the beginning an important centre of Netherlandish sentiment. The philologist Jan Frans WILLEMS (1793–1846) was raised from the position of a humble lawyer's clerk and made assistant archivist of the city of Antwerp. He used his position to stimulate an interest in Flemish literature, wrote of the literary and artistic glory of Flanders, and sought in the history of his own people (the Flemings) those qualities which he thought would establish their future grandeur.

The Flemish bourgeoisie, however, were *not* behind the movement and they viewed with considerable dismay this deliberate fostering of a new pride among the Flemings in their language and culture. The Flemish bourgeoisie were unshaken in their belief in the superiority of the French way of life. They were all French-speaking. They had all grown accustomed to sending their children to be educated in French Catholic boarding schools. And they were in complete agreement with the French-speaking Walloons that Dutch interference in internal Belgian affairs or attempted absorption of Belgium should at all costs be resisted. Together with the Walloons the Flemish bourgeoisie made the revolution of 1830 a reality and gained acceptance from the greater European powers of their right to establish a separate Belgian kingdom whose neutrality was to be guaranteed for all time. They sought not only to dissolve the political union with the Dutch but also to lessen the cultural and linguistic affinity with Holland. Understandably French became the official language of the new kingdom of Belgium. All new laws and regulations were printed and published in French. The Dutch tongue (and its many Flemish variants) was once again relegated to a minor position even in the heart of the Flemish provinces. And Jan Frans Willems, who found himself unable to come to terms with the changed order of things, was deprived of his post in Antwerp and relegated to an insignificant clerkship in the small town of Eekloo, near Ghent, at a quarter of his former salary.

Nothing could have served the nascent Flemish movement

better. For Willems now gave himself up almost entirely to a study of medieval Flemish literature, became a pioneer in Flanders of the literary romanticism which was then sweeping Europe, edited old manuscripts, published medieval romances and wrote local history. By 1836 he felt secure enough to resign his obscure government appointment and moved to Ghent as the natural centre from which to direct his activities. He did for Flanders what the brothers Grimm and Hoffmann von Fallersleben (who was deeply interested in old Flemish and who was in personal contact with Willems) did for Germany. Jacob Grimm published a text of the Flemish Reynart the Fox (which we have already mentioned) and Willems prepared from Grimm's text a modern version of the work which he published in 1834.

In all of this Willems was closely aided by his friend Jan Baptist DAVID (1801–1866). The two had met as students in Antwerp and were from the first drawn together by their common interests in Netherlandish culture. David, however, became a priest, taught in one of the leading colleges in Antwerp, moved to the Catholic seminary in Malines, and then became professor of history and Flemish literature in the Catholic university of Louvain. He used his position to great effect to disseminate Flemish culture to the many Catholic Flemish students who went to Louvain.

Support was also forthcoming from the University of Ghent, and in 1835 the two friends were fortunate in securing a government subsidy for the publication of a Year Book of Flemish Letters. In 1836 the government lent its name to the creation of the 'Société pour le progrès de la langue et de la littérature néerlandaise' and appointed a committee, which included Willems and David among its members, to establish a satisfactory orthography and uniform spelling for Flemish. The report of this committee appeared in 1841, and was enthusiastically adopted at a conference of Flemish writers called in Ghent for the same year: a royal decree of 1844 ordered the immediate implementation of the new system. Two years later Willems was dead, but he lived to see the rights of his cause established and he had brought Flemish writers and intellectuals to recognize the necessity for ridding the Flemish tongue of its dialects and for establishing some measure of discipline and conformity in the use of the language. To him has been rightly attributed the distinction of being the father of the modern Flemish movement.

2

The interest provoked in the Flemish language by Willems and David found ready support from a group of novelists and poets who attempted to preach to the people what the scholars and philologists had uncovered for them. This group, though they wrote much romantic nonsense of only mediocre quality, are important for two reasons: firstly, they succeeded in reviving the glories of Flemish art and rooted their readers in the not undistinguished triumphs of bygone days; secondly, and more important, they paved the way for the greatest and most influential of Flemish romantics, Henri CONSCIENCE (1812–1883).

Henri Conscience was the son of a French sailor who, stationed in Antwerp at the time that Napoleon dreamed of establishing that port as a great naval base, took to himself a wife of pure Flemish stock. Being of indifferent health, the young Henri took no part in the boisterous pastimes of the Antwerp youth of his day but preferred to spend his time in seclusion reading and dreaming over the many Flemish stories that came his way. To complete his education he followed the trend established for other poor boys of intellectual leanings and became a primary school teacher. The revolution of 1830 freed him from what he already regarded as an impossible bondage and enabled him to enlist in the army. When his military career ended in 1836 he was rewarded with a minor official post that gave him the opportunity to write. His first story was in French, but friends urged him to switch to his native tongue, and the soundness of their advice was proved two years later (1838) when *Lion of Flanders*, his masterpiece, met with immediate and conspicuous success.

With a few strokes of the pen Conscience had made the glorious past of Flanders available and intelligible to the simplest mind. And he also gave the Flemish movement its symbol with his creation of the Flemish lion. Inspired by the style of Sir Walter Scott, Conscience took as the theme of his novel the fourteenth-century struggle of the Flemings against the French culminating in their signal and glorious triumph at the Battle of the Golden Spurs (1302). He employed all the exaggeration characteristic of this type of historical romance. He painted everything in glowing colours of heroism and devotion to a worthy cause, and he added the very necessary and somewhat sentimental (if not artificial) love episode. All the characters are depicted with touching and epic simplicity. There is the tender-hearted Mathilde, the ambitious Chatillon, the prudent Deconinck, the courageous Breydel. The two real heroes of the tale, Deconinck the weaver and Breydel the butcher, are incarnations of the people's capacity for conspiracy and revolt, and Deconinck is finally compared to Moses the liberator of the people of Israel. A further character, Thierry the Fox, is lifted boldly from the legend of the 'Quatre Fils Aymon' and is made to disguise himself as Maugis the Magician, miraculously to free prisoners from their cells, and constantly to outwit the most wily of French kings.

This borrowing from familiar folklore was done with deliberate intent to further his avowed aim of making the people read. Similarly his syntax and sentence structure is simple and easily accessible; he uses many gallicisms with which the people would be familiar from everyday usage; he deliberately adopts a rhythmic and archaic style reminiscent of the old epic romances that enables him to avoid a too literary form of Dutch and yet shun the more popular and dialectal modes of expression; and he describes his heroine, Mathilde, in all too familiar sentimental terms: 'Have you seen the fine skeins of gold that are woven in Arabia? Her hair that tumbles in profusion to her heels is purer still and shines no whit the less.'

The next ten years of Conscience's life proved to be very full ones. He published no further historical romances but turned his attention mainly to writing of contemporary village life in the Campine. In 1849, however, came another historical study, this time of the great fourteenth-century Fleming, 'Jacob van Artevelde', and then his pen grew calm again, his style and manner more balanced and realist, his preoccupation with social problems such as pauperism and drink more pronounced. He became administrator of the Brussels museums and realized

in 1869 his ambition of election to the Belgian Academy. Before
he died he had written seventy-one novels and collections of
short stories and had achieved the distinction of seeing his own
monument erected in front of the library at Antwerp with the
inscription: 'He taught his people to read.'

He was at the height of his powers in the 1850's and it is to that
period that belong those works of his (along with his historical
novels) most likely to last. These are *Blind Rosa* (1850), *Rikketik-
ketak* (1851), *The Plague of the Villages* (1853), and *The Miser*
(1856). A last historical novel, *The Strong Men of Flanders*, was
published in 1870. His success was due to a disarming naïveté of
approach, the intensity of his passions, and a consuming sense of
dedication to his purpose. The genius of Conscience lay in that
he realized (however subconsciously) that not only is the Fleming
a great individualist but he is also a great Romantic.
Romanticism suits the Fleming. With him it is not a pose but
part of his nature. He revels in life depicting strong emotions.
He is intrigued by the uncommonly close relationship that must
exist between man and nature along the seashores and amid the
plains of his native province. His consciousness of his exclusion
from the main trends of European life because of his language
focuses his attention in a peculiar way on his social and historical
heritage and gives him a preference for a past that is no longer
true, but a kind of dreamed reality. He believes that passionate
feelings demand a passionate style. Above all, he prefers a poetic
style which is designed to conceal the humdrum and make the
unreal seem real. To all this, in all his writings, Henri Conscience
most faithfully subscribed.

Today it is fashionable to criticize Conscience's too idealistic
conception of life, his often incorrect use of the Flemish tongue,
his lack of technical skill and his most elementary grasp of
character and psychology. None the less he remains great simply
because he was the first novelist to talk to the people at the
people's level and to make them conscious of their nationality
and proud of their race and language. He portrayed faithfully
the life of the humble Fleming, with which he himself was
intimately acquainted and to which he could always be
guaranteed to add an authentic picturesque note. He held
himself aloof from the activities of Flemish extremists such as

Willems and David, generously appreciated the point of view of the French-speaking part of the population even though he might not be able to accept it, and he encouraged the people to adopt an attitude of non-servile respect for those bourgeois classes who, by making Belgium a reality, had given them the possibilities for greatness in their own right as Flemings. He conceived his task as being simply that of teaching the people to read and of arousing in them a love of the good and the beautiful. He became a popular writer and a best-seller. His books were eagerly read by young and old, and were translated into many other European languages. He had a horde of inferior imitators writing both in French and Flemish. And his importance was recognized by Léopold I who not only went out of his way to popularize Conscience's work but also appointed him in 1847 as Flemish tutor to his own children.

3

What Henri Conscience did for the Flemish novel so did Guido GEZELLE (1830–1899) do for Flemish poetry. The son of an original and independent-minded gardener, the young Guido was dispatched from his native Bruges to study at the Catholic seminary at Roulers, to which he returned, after his ordination in 1854, first as a teacher of botany and then to be put in charge of the 'poetry' class (the Sixth Form). His poetic talent first revealed itself by the composition of what were in his day customary effusions to be declaimed at important family gatherings. He proved a most inspiring teacher and quickly gained a devoted following from the more brilliant of his pupils. In 1858 he published two collections of verse: *Poetic Exercises*, which contains those poems written between his eighteenth and twenty-fifth years that he thought worth preserving, and *Churchyard Flowers*, which was inspired primarily by the death of one of his favourite pupils.

What happened next to Gezelle is still a matter for conjecture and we may never know the real truth of the matter. It is certain that he rapidly became as unpopular with his colleagues and the authorities of the seminary as he was popular with his most gifted students. Critics of the early editions of his verse were severe and discouraging, and it was considered odd in the extreme for a priest to write poetry, and of the kind he did write, in a Flemish dialect. For he was not content with the accepted and standardized form of Flemish but insisted on seeking out words and idioms in the dialect of his native West Flanders much as Mistral was doing in Provence to enrich Provençal. He was deliberately fostering a kind of West Flanders regionalism, and he did not conceal the fact that he preferred by far to have Flanders develop its own dialects rather than have them obliterated by the establishment of a standard literary language. Was not this extremist Flemish attitude harmful both to the sons of the Flemish bourgeoisie whom he taught and also to the reputation of the seminary? What could one think of verses such as:

> My Flanders speaks a single tongue,
> God gave each land her own.
> Then be it rich or be it poor,
> It is Flemish and my own!

What again must Gezelle's ecclesiastical superiors have thought of his claim that 'there is a pagan romantic love, but there is also a stronger one, a blessèd half-sacramental Christian friendship . . . *super amorem mulieris*'? What were they to make of 'That Evening and that Rose' (1858), now acknowledged, of course, as one of the best examples of Gezelle's early genius?

> Oh many and many an hour with you
>   I've passed the time with pleasure,
> And never has one hour with you
>   Been less to me than treasure.
> Oh many and many a flower for you
>   To offer you I've plucked
> And like a bee, with you, with you
>   Its honey I have sucked.
> But never an hour so dear with you
>   As long as it could stay,
> And never an hour so sad for you
>   When I must go away,

As the hour when I came close to you
  That evening and sat down
And heard you speak and spoke to you
  Of all our souls had known,
And never a flower was plucked by you
  So beautiful to see
As the one that shone that night on you
  And soon might come to me . . .
And though for me and though for you
  So dear a flower we chose,
A rose, be it even a rose from you,
  Remains not long a rose.
But in my heart I say to you—
  Though how long no man knows—
I keep three well loved pictures: you,
  That evening, and that rose.

(Translated by Clark Stillman)

Gazelle was asked to resign his teaching post in 1860 and students of his probably made matters worse by publishing on their own account a third collection of his verse two years later. Returning to his native Bruges, Gezelle held teaching appointments in schools for English Catholic schoolboys, devoted five strenuous years to popular journalism, and collaborated in the writing of a dictionary of the West Flanders dialect which was published in 1875. From 1870 to 1899 he lived out the remainder of his life obscurely as a parish priest in Courtrai, and now showed himself so hostile to the Flemish movement that many critics have concluded he was under strict orders from his superiors to be so and have even insinuated that he was also forbidden to write poetry.

This is not my view. The lifelike statue that has since been erected to his memory in the market place of Bruges depicts him as an extremely sensitive and withdrawn person. His face, kindly yet marked with what I can only describe as disciplined compassion, has that haunting look of one who has had to resolve alone a deep personal conflict. The harsh and abrupt dismissal from Roulers not only disappointed and discouraged him but was also deeply wounding. It was only slowly that he could recover from such a shock. And I think it significant that, once the dictionary was published, he cautiously felt his way back to his true vocation as a poet. In 1878 he issued an indifferent volume made up of earlier unpublished work, and he also gave permission for his three earlier books to appear in eagerly awaited new editions. Encouraged by their enthusiastic reception, he took up his pen once again and there appeared in 1893 *Crown of Time*, in 1897 *Necklace of Rhymes*, and (posthumously) in 1902 *Last Verses*.

Gezelle's choice of subject matter was as commonplace and as simple, direct and unaffected as his style. He was a nature poet, but above all he was a religious poet who knew how to express his faith in lyrical poems which made their instant impact and permanent appeal:

> How noble, beautiful and good
> Can be a simple flower bud,
> That suddenly, as if unplanned,
> Springs from its Creator's hand!
>
> Through Him and through no human sowing
> Came this humble seed to growing;
> Through Him, this moment of this day
> It bloomed and comfort came my way.

Everything about him for ever reminds him of God's goodness to man, and his sense of the Divine is at times so absolute as to qualify almost for the label of Pantheist. He identifies himself in an almost Wordsworthian sense with the life of the country people about him. He thinks *in* song and the profound melancholy that he constantly experiences is only assuaged by song:

> O Song, O Song,
> You help the pain
> When grief strikes, and disaster—
> O Song, the wounded heart again
> Grows whole when you are master . . .

And in his latest period he proves to be a profound and devout mystic whilst still retaining his spontaneity and purity of utterance:

O Lord, Thou lov'st in us alone
thy own, thy very being,
which in all things is thousandfold
imprinted for our reading. . . .

And we, in all that's lovable
'tis Thee we shall be loving,
and have, O God, in Thee alone
our end and our beginning.

Gezelle's technique is free from all traditional forms of expression. He resorts frequently to *enjambement*; he uses alliteration and onomatopoeia with telling effect; he strives constantly to achieve the correct balance and the melodious phrase; and, for the most part, unlike so many lyrical poets, he remains refreshingly detached and objective. In his first period of activity he was mainly read and appreciated in his beloved West Flanders. When, in his second period, he displayed a more mature and spontaneous style, the derogatory views of earlier critics changed to almost extravagant praise, and he came to be acclaimed both in Holland and Flanders as Flanders' greatest poet. This he undoubtedly was, and later generations of Flemish poets have had cause to be grateful to him, not only for striking a new and authentic Flemish note but also for making the Flemings themselves poetry-conscious. His moving 'Prayer for Compassion' has been heard and answered:

Have compassion!
Much I sang and now am still,
    (Have compassion!)
Now no longer can or will
    (Have compassion)
Sing again; I am resigned,
    (Have compassion)
Old and poor and almost blind.
    (Have compassion!)

4

Belgian literature of French expression had to await the new impetus demanded of it by the earlier politicians of the new kingdom until Charles De Coster (1827–1879) produced his *Ulenspiegel*. Schooled though these politicians were in a traditional French outlook, they were far-sighted enough to be aware of the necessity for bringing about as complete a separation as possible from French cultural ties, and their ablest spokesman, J. B. Nothomb, was already reminding his fellow-countrymen as early as 1833 of their duties in this direction. To achieve political independence alone, he argued, was not enough. There must be a similar rebirth of Belgian intellectual life. It was the duty of all to remember that

> placée entre l'Allemagne, la France et l'Angleterre, la Belgique peut s'attribuer une mission particulière; qu'elle se garde de se faire vassal politique ou littéraire d'une de ces nations. Pourquoi puiserait-elle aux seules sources intellectuelles de la France, de cette France qui, elle-même, va se retremper en Allemagne? Qu'elle fasse des emprunts à ces trois grandes sociétés intelligentes. Si elle les fait avec discernement et impartialité, elle paraîtra déjà originale; elle le sera véritablement si elle veut se rappeler son passé qui ne fut ni sans éclat ni sans grandeur.[1]

It was surely a happy coincidence that at the very moment Nothomb was exhorting the Belgians to seek their artistic inspiration amid their own colourful and turbulent past, a small boy who was later to realize to the full Nothomb's dream was making his way from his birthplace, Munich, to begin his education at the hands of the Jesuits in the Collège Saint Michel in Brussels! Charles de Coster, though born in Munich where his father was intendant to the Papal Nuncio, was of pure Belgian stock. His studies at the Collège Saint Michel seem to have been in no way distinguished, and on leaving school he found a modest but secure employment in the bank of the Société Générale. His lonely, restless spirit, however, soon revolted against business orthodoxy, as it revolted against the Catholic orthodoxy of his day. By 1850 he was enrolled as a student of law at the free-thinking University of Brussels, and he graduated some five years later. In the meantime, he had founded in 1847 with a number of friends the *Société des Joyeux*, and his first literary efforts appeared in the bulletins issued by this enthusiastic

[1] quoted by Pirenne: *Histoire de Belgique*, tome vii, Brussels, 1932, p. 258

group of young Brussels intellectuals. As more important periodicals appeared he found in them a market for his writings, but the really decisive step in his career came when Félicien Rops started a weekly with the significant title of *Uylenspiegel* and enrolled him as a contributor.

Between 1856 and 1864 he wrote regularly on political matters for this review and contributed short stories and sketches, many of which were to form the basis of his *Légendes Flamandes* (published 1858) and his *Contes Brabançonnes* (1861). Perhaps at this early period in his career he was at his happiest. He loved with gusto and ingenuous abandon. He loved life. He loved his native land. He loved the warmth and brooding passion of contemporary German literature as he despised what he termed the cold and distant cynicism of French style. And he loved Elisa Spruyt. To this young woman he unburdened himself freely, and one remarkable letter written to her in 1852 clearly depicts what formative influences were then at work:

> J'ai une passion pour les Allemands . . . j'aime toute cette littérature pensive, douce, pleine de cœur et de passion, qui fait si bien rêver ; j'aime ses poètes qui savent si bien peindre l'amour comme je le rêve . . . La littérature française, au contraire, c'est la littérature du doute, c'est le mépris profond de la femme, avec des flatteries de chien couchant, c'est l'homme sans cœur parlant de sentiments, qu'il n'a jamais éprouvés, c'est l'homme que rien ne remue et qui n'aime qu'une chose, parler et parler bien. L'Allemand souffre, pense et rêve, il est artiste au fond du cœur, il aime d'amour tout ce qui est beau; le laid le fait souffrir, le mal l'indigne, la blague le révolte.[1]

Shortly after leaving the university he secured an important but ill-paid job as member of a commission established to publish as complete a collection as possible of the ancient laws and usages of the country, and he devoted four years of his life to this task – four decisive and formative years in that they compelled him to pore over countless ancient manuscripts, particularly of the sixteenth century, and so gave him the background and feeling for style necessary for the eventual success of his

[1] *Lettres à Elisa*, Brussels, 1894: a posthumous publication prepared by a distinguished critic, Charles Potvin.

masterpiece, *La Légende et les Aventures héroïques, joyeuses et glorieuses d'Ulenspiegel et de Lamme Goedzak au pays de Flandre et ailleurs.*

This book, usually referred to as *Thyl Ulenspiegel*, or quite simply *Ulenspiegel*, was first published in 1867 and at the time attracted little attention. By now, his unhappy love affair with Elisa Spruyt was at an end, and he had separated from his mother and sister to live as a poor recluse in the suburbs of Brussels, visited only by a handful of friends and supporters who believed firmly in his genius and importance. Through their kindly influence he secured in 1870 a modest position as teacher of literature in the Brussels Military Academy. He gave French lessons to young English women. He lectured sporadically up and down the country. He published a further novel, *Le Voyage de Noces* (1872), his impressions of a journey through Holland (*La Zélande*, 1874), and a short story 'Le Mariage de Toulet' (1879). He died, poor and still unnoticed, in this latter year, tended only in his garret bedroom by a woman to whom he in turn had charitably given shelter.

Genius in a garret! If ever an example were needed to give the lie to the cosy, romantic notion of what fun all this can be, surely that example is to be found in the profoundly unhappy existence of Charles de Coster. To argue that it was largely his own fault and that he could have had an assured if modest existence as a bank clerk is to evade the issue. His was a spirit of revolt against orthodoxy, against prim, bourgeois platitudes, against the complacency of his times. In all his political writings he betrayed his hostility to the Church and its traditional teaching. He wanted no return to the middle ages conception of domination of the people by the clergy. Individual liberty, for which the Belgians had for centuries fought, was a sacred and inalienable right. When in 1857 a storm broke out over the administration of legacies and donations for charitable purposes (the 'loi des couvents'), and the Catholic government of the day passed legislation favourable to the Church, Charles de Coster was a determined antagonist, and a supporter of the demonstrations that finally led to the collapse of the government. All his literary work bore the stamp also of this passionate championing of the people's rights and privileges, and it is well to remember that the turbulent period between 1860 and 1870 that marked a growing hostility to the Papacy and a defiance of Napoleon III (who had set himself up as the protector of the Vatican) was for de Coster a gestatory period leading to the production of *Thyl Ulenspiegel*. *Ulenspiegel*, indeed, represents the struggle of joyous living against asceticism and oppression; the struggle of the Belgian people against Spain; it is an epic of the people, always overrun yet never crushed or subdued; it deals with the people's laughter and tears, its dramas and revolts. The spirit of Claes, the father of Thyl, still smoulders in the heart of every true Belgian, and also in the heart of every individual who would be called a 'man'. Hence, in part at least, the reason for the universal appeal of the book and its translation into several other languages.

As with many geniuses, however, de Coster was ahead of his times and this explains both the contemporary neglect of his work and his rapidly increasing popularity as the nineteenth century drew to a close. *Ulenspiegel*, and also to a less marked degree his earlier publications, introduced stylistic innovations and represented a rebellion against the Parisian academics and the mediocre and pedestrian novelists who turned themselves into bad imitators of Sir Walter Scott, or of the popular Flemish writer, Henri Conscience. In this sense, de Coster did for French literature in Belgium what Conscience did for Flemish. Both were intensely nationalistic. Both resisted French influences. Both, in their different methods of approach, spoke to and for the people of Belgium. De Coster, however, ardently followed the German romantic movement; admired Goethe and Schiller; approved the pattern set by Scott, Walpole and Byron, and faithfully copied by the Germans, of glorifying the past at the expense of the smug and self-satisfied present and so high-lighting heroic and nationalistic qualities of mind, attitude and character that tended to be submerged and neglected amid the chicanery of the times.

His studies at the University of Brussels and the work he did for the royal commission on the publication of ancient laws and usages in Belgium determined his style and gave him the period and setting for *Ulenspiegel*. The language he uses is curious, archaic, limpid. It is inherited from the chroniclers of the sixteenth century, and is also strongly reminiscent of Rabelais, of Montaigne, and of the Balzac of the *Contes Drolatiques*. It represents the generous fury of a man, or even of a whole race, revolting against tyrants. It has an irresistible drollness. It is sustained by a burning desire to exalt truth, come what may. Violent and brutal images are placed in rapid juxtaposition and conveyed by impulsive and dazzling turns of phrase. And the effect is such that as we read we are reminded again and again of the paintings of the sixteenth-century Flemish artist, Bruegel: of his 'Triomphe de la Mort'; of his 'Danse des Paysans'; of his drinking parties and scenes of quiet domesticity and children's games and golden harvests. For the rich, bold colours of Bruegel and his telling and often repellent detail we have de Coster's sweep of imagery and his limpid and clear prose. The following description, for example, is pure Bruegel. The boy Philip, son of the Emperor Charles V and the future Philip II, is engaged in slowly burning to death a young monkey he had received as a present – a grim reminder of the shape of things to come:

> La bestiole avait tant souffert en mourant dans ce feu que son petit corps semblait être, non pas celui d'un animal ayant eu vie, mais un fragment de racine rugueuse et tordue, et dans sa bouche ouverte comme pour crier la mort, se voyait de l'écume sanglante, et l'eau de ses larmes mouillait sa face.

We are then told that Charles V, furious,

> allait battre son fils pissant de peur, quand l'archevêque l'arrêtant lui dit à l'oreille: Son Altesse sera un jour grande brûleuse d'hérétiques. – L'empereur sourit, et tous deux sortirent, laissant l'enfant seul avec sa guenon. Mais il en était d'autres qui n'étaient point des guenons et mouraient dans des flammes.

The importance rightly accorded to *Ulenspiegel* should not, however, lead us to consider the earlier works as negligible. *Les Légendes Flamandes* and *Contes Brabançonnes* can still be highly entertaining, and the former work in particular clearly points the way to *Ulenspiegel* and begins shaping the style for the later masterpiece. The story of Smetse Smee, for example. Smetse Smee is a blacksmith from Ghent who has dared to oppose the Spanish Inquisition. In consequence, he is a poor and ruined man. On the point of committing suicide he is approached by the Devil and signs with him a seven-year pact. Immediately, clients and fortune are his. But he is now profoundly unhappy and increasingly dreads the fatal day of reckoning. Suddenly, the Holy Family descends on his house and demands hospitality. Generously and reverently he entertains them, and in return is freed from his pact with the Devil and granted three wishes. At the end of three successive periods of seven years he is allowed to immobilize on a tree, in a chair, and tied up in a sack, three individuals of his own choice. His choice in turn falls upon, first, the inquisitor Jacob Hessels for the tree, secondly the Duke of Alba for the chair, and thirdly Philip II of Spain for the sack. Smetse Smee then lives on to the ripe old age of 93, and dies poor but content. He is, however, held up at the gates of Paradise and conceives the project of opening a tavern there. Furious, Saint Peter tries to drive him away, but Jesus himself intervenes and allows him to stay. Has not Smetse Smee been a generous, hard-working, good and jovial fellow? Has he not been a life-long and valiant protagonist for liberty of conscience? And has he not triumphed over the three worst enemies the fair land of Flanders has had to contend with?

The origins of Charles de Coster's Thyl Ulenspiegel are obscure, but he is by tradition a half-Flemish half-Germanic character of peasant origin who lived some time during the fourteenth century and who died, according to tradition, near Lübeck in 1350. In all the earlier manuscripts he is, as the derived French word accurately describes him, *espiègle*. He is a mischievous character, without malice or wickedness, but delighting in interpreting all orders he receives literally, or carrying them out in reverse with a great show of mock docility and much fooling. He stoops without hesitation to scurrility and obscenity. His jests are often coarsely practical and he exercises his wit and roguery not only on the tradespeople of the towns and the innkeepers, but also on priests, noblemen and princes. In English literature he is associated with Robin Goodfellow, and Ben Jonson refers to him in *The Alchemist* as 'Howleglass' and 'Ulenspiegel'. If we are to believe the critic Potvin, Charles de Coster discovered his Thyl in a translation into French of a book written by an Antwerp merchant, Van Meteren, in 1618 and bearing the title *Histoire des Pays-Bas . . . depuis l'an 1315 jusques à l'an 1612.* It is improbable, however, that de Coster was not already familiar with some variants of the legend of Ulenspiegel that were published as early as 1478, and in particular from Strasbourg in 1515 and again in 1519. What attracted de Coster in particular to the *Histoire des Pays-Bas* was this Flemish merchant's strong nationalist feelings and his eloquent plea for liberty, all of which he managed subtly to conceal amid his prolixities on navigation, travel, foreign exchange, linguistics, and the like. Ultimately, of course, de Coster brought his own process of alchemy to work and distilled from the legendary stories and from Van Meteren his own particular brand of hero, making him a truly Belgian national figure and causing him to typify the resistance of both Flemings and Walloons against the Spanish yoke.

Thyl Ulenspiegel comprises in all five books. The first deals with the pranks of the young Thyl at the period when Charles V's reign was drawing to a close. The second book concerns itself with the government of the Duke of Alba, with the inquisition in the lowlands, and with the various defeats of William of Orange. The third describes the adventures of the *Gueux des Bois*, friends of the peasants and the poor, and sworn enemies of the monks. The fourth book shows Thyl an active participant in the attacks of the armed fleet – *Les Gueux de Mer* – against the Spaniards in the lowlands in 1571. Lastly, we assist at the proclamation of the United Netherlands, the assassination of William of Orange at Philip II's instigation to bring to an end this short-lived period of independence, the apparent death of Thyl at the same time, and his triumphant resurrection. The allegorical intent is clear.

The birth and whole life of Thyl is shown by de Coster to be the very antithesis of that of Philip II of Spain:

> A Damme, en Flandre, quand Mai ouvrait leurs fleurs aux aubépines, naquit Ulenspiegel, fils de Claes. Une commère sage femme et nommée Katheline l'enveloppa de langes chaudes, et, lui ayant regardé la tête, y montra une peau. – Coiffé, né sous une bonne étoile! – dit-elle joyeusement.

And later: 'Tandis que croissait en gaie malice le fils vaurien du charbonnier, végétait en maigre mélancolie le rejeton dolent du sublime empereur.'

The one is the personification of tyranny, cruelty, and tight-lipped bigotry. The other is gay, free as air, a generous and warm-hearted vagabond.

Thus, at the same time that the future Philip II was being born in luxury in Spain, Thyl was likewise born at Damme. His father, Claes, and his mother, Soetkin, were poor and from an early age Thyl knew hardship and treachery – for this was the period when denunciations to the Spanish Inquisition began to be frequent. Yet Thyl was a smiling and charming rogue, and in love with Nele, the bastard daughter of Katheline, the midwife:

> . . . Ulenspiegel et Nele s'aimaient d'amour. . . . Nele se tenait au bras d'Ulenspiegel et de ses deux mains s'y accrochait. Ulenspiegel prenant plaisir à ce jeu, passait souvent son bras autour de la taille de Nele, pour la mieux tenir, disait-il. Et elle était heureuse, mais elle n'en parlait point. Le vent roulait mollement sur les chemins le parfum des prairies; la mer au loin mugissait au soleil, paresseuse; Ulenspiegel était comme un jeune diable, tout fier, et Nele, comme une petite sainte du Paradis toute honteuse de son plaisir. Elle appuyait sa tête sur l'épaule d'Ulenspiegel, il lui prenait les mains et, cheminant, il la baisait au front, sur les joues et sur sa bouche mignonne.

Naturally, such a charming idyll cannot last. Unjustly condemned for a crime of heresy, Thyl finds himself banished for three years and obliged to make a pilgrimage to Rome to buy his pardon for the sum of seven florins. On his travels he discovers that criminals prosper everywhere and that the innocent alone suffer. He has to replace the jester whose job it is to make Philip laugh. Engaged as the emperor's trumpeter, he deliberately omits to herald that monarch's arrival. He joins forces with Lamme Goedzak who is in search of his wife who has deserted him. In Hamburg he sells horse droppings at fifty florins a bag, calling them seeds of prophecy. With the Landgrave of Hesse he pretends to be a painter, executes a fresco and says that the ugly among his clients will not see their true image but only a blank wall. In Nuremberg he passes himself off as a doctor and cures a whole hospital by the simple expedient of announcing that all the truly sick will be burned alive. And so, finally, he comes back to his native land.

Here, tragedy awaits him. Katheline the midwife, having been condemned as a witch and tortured, has gone mad. His father, Claes, is arrested as a heretic and burned at the stake. At the dead of night Thyl creeps to the scene of execution, gathers together a few ashes that remain, wraps them preciously in a piece of red and black silk, wears them next to his own heart, and proclaims them 'le feu de vengeance contre les bourreaux'. Then follows a simple and moving description of the break-up of Thyl's home, a masterpiece of understatement that conveys all the more poignantly the numb despair of Soetkin:

> Soetkin voyait de chez Katheline descendre le berceau de fer et de cuivre qui, de père en fils, avait toujours été dans la maison de Claes, où le pauvre mort était né, où était né aussi Ulenspiegel. Puis ils descendirent le lit où Soetkin avait conçu son enfant et où elle avait passé de si douces nuits sur l'épaule de son homme. Puis vint aussi la huche où elle serrait le pain, le bahut où étaient les viandes au temps de fortune, des poêles, chaudrons et coquasses non plus luisants comme au temps de bonheur, mais souillés de la poussière de l'abandon.

Mother and son are in turn tortured, and poor Soetkin succumbs. Thyl and Nele drink a magic philtre and in a dream invoke the gods to save Flanders from the oppressor. 'Find the seven!' is the only answer they receive. An even longer odyssey now begins for Thyl. He becomes a messenger for William of Orange, recruits soldiers for him, prints Protestant bibles, kills papists, runs his own peculiar form of guerilla warfare, plays his pranks on authority, and finally joins the Sea Beggars who bring William of Orange victory at La Brielle on 1 April 1572. His good friend Lamme has been with him all this time, still in search of his errant wife, and he finally discovers her as mistress of a monk whom he fattens up and pardons, for 'c'est l'heure des légitimes amours'. Naturally, Nele has also joined Thyl in this later period.

A kind of *mystique* now pervades the last section of the work. The two lovers, still in the prime of youth, go off together and take still another magic philtre. In another dream they are transported to the islands of the birds and there the gods reveal to them the meaning of the 'seven' they were earlier commanded to find. It is a question of the seven capital sins: pride, avarice, anger, gluttony, envy, sloth and luxury – which are now for the tried and blessèd turned into seven essential virtues: pride of spirit, thrift, zest for life, energy, honest competition, *rêverie*, and love. In fact, qualities of mind and heart that any patriotic Belgian would be anxious to claim as characteristic of his race. After his death, Thyl rises from the sands that have covered his grave and vanishes for ever with Nele into the never-never land.

The main defect of the book – if in a work of this kind it may be called a defect – is that there are three parallel threads of action that can never properly fuse at any given point: the picaresque adventures of Thyl, the historical incidents into which he is cast, and the symbolical and dream-like settings. But then, this is an epic conceived on a grand scale, and like all epics sets out to be nothing more than a rich mosaic of loosely connected and independent incidents. It is also a fairy story in the best traditions of the past: of Cinderella, Jack the Giant Killer, Tom Thumb; of the triumph of the weak but valiant over the mighty and unjust; of the ordinary people in both joy and tribulation asserting their right to be free. To attack de Coster, as some critics have done, for his archaisms and his deliberate pastiche of sixteenth-century French is again unwarranted. Over long and patient years he forged for himself the only possible vehicle of expression capable of telling his story as he wanted it to be told.

Neglected and misunderstood though he was at the time he wrote, his influence has been both salutary and pervasive. He forced later writers to cultivate a robust and personal style more suited to their national temper and therefore more satisfying artistically than following palely in the wake of Parisian fashion. In a sense, he made possible Verhaeren, whose role it was to glorify not the past but the present and the future. He made possible Camille Lemonnier, who believed firmly in the existence of a particular Belgian temperament, who tried to portray it in all his stories, and who openly acknowledged his indebtedness to de Coster. 'C'est en de Coster,' he wrote in *La Vie Belge*, 'que je reconnus le véritable homme de ma lignée.' Georges Eekhoud's hostility against the greedy and egotistical bourgeoisie, the Flemish background he chooses for his writings, and his powerful descriptions of the rude existence and primitive passions of the people of Antwerp in his epic novel, *La Nouvelle Carthage* (1888) – all this is in line of descent from de Coster. Again, could Maeterlinck have given us *L'Oiseau Bleu* (1908) without the example of Thyl and Nele to show him that such a journey was worth the making?

The group of young writers who founded the movement *La Jeune Belgique* in 1881 were all enthusiastic in their praise of de Coster and in acknowledging the importance of the lead he had given them. 'Be yourselves! Root yourselves in your native soil and take to yourselves all it has to offer.' Such, in effect, had been his message. 'Soyons Nous' was the motto these young writers chose for themselves. With them came a real literary revival. Largely through their influence *Thyl Ulenspiegel* achieved the success it deserved. The first cheap and popular editions appeared in 1893. It has gone on delighting young and old alike ever since.

CHAPTER TWO

La Jeune Belgique

I

BY THE time that Belgium was ready to celebrate fifty years of independence with an impressive exhibition young men as full of ideas as of sound and fury were thronging the four flourishing universities the country now boasted and clamouring to be heard. They were all from the leisured bourgeois class, they were all well schooled in the French tongue (even though their names so often betrayed their Flemish origin), and they were at the university to please their parents, to study law and to amuse themselves. But they were both perceptive and intelligent, and if their amusement took the form of publishing a wide variety of student reviews and magazines it also led them to be highly critical of the background from which they came and in idealistic revolt against their own class. It equally led a number of them to find their true vocation in literature rather than in law – a tendency, be it noted, that has perpetuated itself down to the present.

These young lawyers found themselves belonging to a class and taking economic support from a system for which they had only contempt. The bourgeois (and Liberal) right to govern seemed no longer divinely ordained. Bourgeois patronage could no longer be deemed sufficient for the needs of society as a whole. Their faith in bourgeois institutions correspondingly declined. They sensed that the social order in which they had been reared was already involved in a rapid decline in power. A growing feeling of guilt and malaise gave these well-connected young men a social consciousness (not necessarily a social conscience) that demanded expression in one form or another and which also gave rise to a democratic spirit much in sympathy with the aspirations of the growing working-class movement. The mistake must not be made, however, of thinking that the inspiration of the writers amongst this younger generation was rooted in the socialist revolution that was taking place. It so happened – and history has many examples to offer us – that the two movements were coincident.[1] True, a few of the writers did give their attention to socialism, to journalism or to religion, but their literary output then practically ceased.

Between 1874 and 1884 no fewer than twenty-five literary reviews made their appearance, many of them of humble origin at the whim of small student groups, a number destined to share the fate of most little reviews and perish after the initial impetus had spent itself, a few of outstanding importance in that they provided a teething period for many writers who were later to be famous. Most of these reviews – which had their own literary côterie in such diverse places as Brussels, Ghent, Louvain, Verviers, Mons, Liège and Antwerp – finally merged with the Brussels *Jeune Revue* (1880), and this in turn became in 1881 *La Jeune Belgique* which, under the inspired editorship of Max Waller, grouped together some of the most significant names amongst the younger generation. It is with the contributors to *La Jeune Belgique*, and also with the fortunes of its great rival *La Wallonie* (founded in Liège in 1886) that we shall be principally concerned in this chapter.

2

In 1880 a group of young lawyers gathered themselves about a veteran colleague, Edmond PICARD (1836–1924), to found a new review to be entitled *L'Art Moderne*. Edmond Picard was not only the close friend of the novelist Camille Lemonnier, but also an essayist and minor poet of some reputation, and a distinguished barrister. He combined a combative spirit with a definite charm and a domineering gift for friendship. He was also unusual, and

[1] It should be remembered that a not dissimilar movement among the sons of the well-to-do occurred in Germany at about the same time. This culminated in the founding of the *Wandervögel* who, in the opinion of one authority, were the forerunners of the National Socialist movement. Though they were not a literary group, the *Wandervögel* similarly stressed the spiritual freedom of the individual and wished to turn their backs on the moral inertia of the established order.

therefore attractive to the younger generation, in that he had spent two years at sea (signing on as an ordinary seaman and then achieving the rank of second lieutenant) between leaving school and going on to the university to study law. In founding *L'Art Moderne* he enunciated the principle that all art must be useful to social progress – this as a counterblast to Théophile Gautier's doctrine of 'l'art pour l'art' – and he proposed to attack the strangehold of the French theatre in Belgium, to favour the development of a purely national theatre, and to promote by all the means in his power a truly national literary revival. The first number of *L'Art Moderne* appeared in March 1881.

Meanwhile, two excitable young men had fallen foul of the university authorities of Louvain for the tempestuous nature of their literary discussions and had had their student publications suppressed. One of them, Emile Verhaeren, came immediately as a junior to the law chambers of Edmond Picard and was therefore an early contributor to *L'Art Moderne*. The other, Max WALLER (1860–1889), took over the editorship of what was to be called *La Jeune Belgique* and received backing and support from Edmond Picard and from *L'Art Moderne*. The first number of *La Jeune Belgique* appeared in December 1881, and it was immediately obvious that a major literary event had occurred and that Max Waller was an editor of unusual skill, ability and drive. Albert Giraud, Georges Eekhoud, Georges Rodenbach, Emile Verhaeren, Jules Destrée and Iwan Gilkin were among his early contributors – all of them at that time completely unknown – and they formed an eager, campaigning coterie.

Though *Les Jeunes Belgiques*, as they called themselves, had no clearly defined programme, they voiced general discontent with the literary past of their country and were enraged at the neglect of the few great writers they considered Belgium had produced: De Coster, Octave Pirmez and Camille Lemonnier. They also considered that the poet André VAN HASSELT (1806–1874), friend, disciple and imitator of Victor Hugo, had been unjustly neglected; that, though his output was uneven and his style often too declamatory, he was the most important Romantic poet Belgium had had; that as a precursor he was in the truest tradition that Belgian verse of French expression should follow. All these early views of the contributors to Max Waller's review met with the full support of Edmond Picard, and he generously invited them to dine with him each Sunday at his home and discuss with him their plans and projects.

They were even more riotously welcome at the home of Camille Lemonnier, to whom Max Waller had presented the first few numbers of *La Jeune Belgique*. Camille Lemonnier placed no guiding reins on these young men, was more understanding than Edmond Picard, and did not seek to direct them. Friday night, therefore, became 'the master's night', and after wining and dining with Lemonnier the group argued fiercely, lengthily and loudly in his company until the early hours of the morning. Gradually they became classified as standing for Lemonnier and Naturalism in prose works and for Baudelaire and the Parnassians in poetry. Max Waller consistently attacked bourgeois pomposity and self-complacency; wrote sarcastic and scathing articles against Goethe's *Faust*, against the teaching of literature in the universities, and in praise of Naturalism; he sang the glory of Lemonnier and of his own new poets, Eekhoud, Rodenbach and Hannon. He seized every opportunity he could to attack the public for its stupidity and its indifference to literature. In short, he created a 'stir'. Nor did the enthusiasm of these militant youngsters end with the printed word. Max Waller lectured in Brussels. Verhaeren gave a series of lectures in Flanders on the revival of Belgian letters. Rodenbach toured the whole country, compelling attention with his charm and warmth of personality, and dinning into the minds of his audiences that Belgium had two important categories of writers who must be honoured. In the first and more important category he placed 'les grands dieux' – De Coster, Picard, Pirmez and Lemonnier. Into his second category ('les dieux inférieurs') fell naturally Waller, Eekhoud, Giraud and Verhaeren. It was, of course, a blatant piece of self-advertisement the like of which had never been heard of before in Belgium. It was a literary blast, and like all such blasts puffed the indifferent or mediocre alongside those who were to be truly great.[1]

---

[1] The closest parallel to be found in England is the Auden-Isherwood group of the 1930's and the launching of John Lehmann's *New Writing*.

3

Thus, Théo HANNON (1851–1916) was never more than a talented and pretty versifier. Jules DESTRÉE (1863–1936) soon threw in his lot with the Socialist party, achieved fame as a barrister and some reputation as an art critic, and as Socialist minister for Science and the Arts was instrumental in 1920 in promoting the foundation of the *Académie Royale de Langue et de Littérature françaises*. Iwan GILKIN (1858–1924) never fulfilled his early promise, was too hesitant and groping, too obsessed with Parnassian perfection of style, and too morbidly fascinated by Baudelaire's *Fleurs du Mal*. His best work was probably done in the theatre, that medium being most suited to his penchant for treating important historical and sociological events on a grand scale. Octave PIRMEZ (1832–1883), the melancholic dreamer, the recluse and country gentleman, could hardly be placed in the same class as de Coster or Lemonnier. Influenced by his deep reading of Montaigne, Pascal, Rousseau, Chateaubriand, Pirmez' chief claim to fame today resides perhaps in the influence he in turn had on Georges Rodenbach and Fernand Séverin. In his *Heures de Philosophie* (1873) he states clearly his position when he writes:

La raison, faculté moyenne, chemine d'un pas assuré; mais le sentiment, faculté presque divine, voltige et plane dans l'immensité sur les ailes de l'amour.

Georges EEKHOUD (1854–1927), on the other hand, quickly developed as a novelist, short story writer and journalist. He forged for himself an intensely vigorous and hard-hitting style admirably suited to the subjects he loved to treat: the passionate and often brutal lives of the poor and under-privileged living in the desolate and dune-covered wastes of the Campine, in Flanders. He makes a kind of cult of the toiling masses whom he venerates with pantheistic devotion. He is, in fact, in several ways, in direct line with the late Russian novelist, Maxim Gorky. His best work is undoubtedly his epic novel about the port of Antwerp, *La Nouvelle Carthage* (1888); his *Kermesses* (1884) and

Nouvelles Kermesses (1887); and his translations of Webster's
Duchess of Malfi (1890), of Beaumont and Fletcher's *Philaster, or
Love Lies A-Bleeding* (1895), of Marlowe's *Edward II* (1896).

Albert GIRAUD (1860-1929) developed as a poet in the pure
Parnassian tradition, a rare stylist, more Latin than Belgian in
mentality, yet still with a deep attachment to his native country.
Mockel summed him up as being a poet of will rather than of
instinct, and, reproaching Verhaeren for what he termed his
artistic laxity, averred the contrary for Giraud who betrayed 'un
excès de tenue dans l'ordre si pur de la forme'. In other words,
Giraud was a greater stylist than he was a poet. Artistic
integrity meant everything to him. He strongly attacked Picard's
thesis that all art must be useful to social progress, and he
became increasingly polemical and more and more intractable
in expressing his opinions. The publication of *Le Laurier* (1919),
comprising his collected verse of the agonizing war years,
reminded the public of the intense love he had for his native
country. His last volume, *Le Concert dans un Musée* (1925) gives us
perhaps the most intimate approach to the poet we can hope for:

> Ecoute la chanson du beau pays de Flandre!
> Prières de dévote à l'ombre d'un pilier,
> Voix de l'heure qui traîne et voudrait faire attendre.
> Ecoute-la passer, la chanson rauque et tendre,
> L'instant de retourner son naïf sablier.
> La plus douce à mon cœur de toutes les chansons!...
> Mais qui n'est pas d'ici ne peut pas la comprendre!

4

One unkind critic has said of Georges RODENBACH (1855-
1898) that perhaps the most important thing he ever did was to
popularize the city of Bruges as a tourist centre! Surely a more
important claim to fame is that he was the first of a distinguished
group of young writers, all pure Flemings, all of whom not only
came from Ghent but were also educated on the same benches in
the Jesuit college of Sainte-Barbe, and that he, Rodenbach, took
it upon himself to present three of these writers for the first time

to the public in the pages of *La Jeune Belgique* (5 July 1886). Their
names were Grégoire Le Roy, Charles Van Lerberghe, and
Maurice Maeterlinck!

It was whilst reading law at the University of Ghent that
Georges Rodenbach prepared his first volume of verse, much in
the Romantic tradition, obviously influenced by François
Coppée, and entitled *Le Foyer et les Champs* (1877). He took a
year's holiday in Paris (1878–1879), came to Brussels determined
to abandon law for literature, threw in his lot with *La Jeune
Belgique*, published another collection of verse (*La Jeunesse
Blanche*, 1886), and two years later returned for good to Paris
where he matured and produced his best work. *Le Règne du
Silence* (1891) deals with the same Flemish themes as his earlier
collections of verse, betrays his indebtedness to Baudelaire and
Verlaine, and in an elaborate style evokes a nostalgic and
melancholy past:

> En province dans la langueur matutinale,
> Tinte le carillon, tinte la douceur
> De l'aube qui regarde avec des yeux de sœur,
> Tinte le carillon, – et sa musique pâle
> S'effeuille fleur à fleur sur les toits d'alentour,
> Et sur les escaliers des pignons noirs s'effeuille
> Comme un bouquet de sons mouillés que le vent cueille!
> Musique du matin qui tombe de la tour,
> Qui tombe de très loin en guirlandes fanées,
> Qui tombe de Naguère en invisibles lis,
> En pétales si lents, si froids, et si pâlis,
> Qu'ils semblent s'effeuiller du front mort des Années!

Of the four novels and numerous short stories he then wrote,
all dealing with similar Flemish backgrounds, all dreamily
evoking memories of chiming bells, tall steeples, blue-slated
roofs, the timelessness and peace and calm of the red-brick
enclosures of the *béguines*, *Bruges-La-Morte* (1892) is the most
successful and deservedly the most popular. In this novel he gave
himself the task, as he put it, of becoming 'le peintre de cette ville
morte comme Turner le fut de Venise', and he succeeded
triumphantly. For Rodenbach, Bruges was an 'état d'âme', and
this he set out to capture by making it the pivot on which the

simple action of the novel turns. His hero, Hugues, lives all alone in his house on the Quai du Rosaire, mourning his wife who died some ten years ago and jealously guarding tresses of her once luxuriant hair in pious veneration. He feels almost in mystic communion with this dead, silent city, for 'Bruges était sa morte. Et sa morte était Bruges.' One day he meets a girl dancer, Jane Scott, and because she reminds him of his wife he begins a long and drawn-out affair with her. At long last he takes Jane home. All the pageantry of the religious procession of the Holy Blood is about to take place. Jane wishes to show herself and to see the procession. A quarrel ensues. Inadvertently Jane touches *his* relic! Beside himself he snatches the tresses of hair from her and with them strangles her.

5

Camille LEMONNIER (1844–1913) was, as we have already noted, the acknowledged 'master' of all these youngsters and the fortunes of *La Jeune Belgique* soon centred on the controversies surrounding him. Lemonnier had been an obvious choice to deliver the funeral oration on Charles de Coster in 1879, and between 1879 and 1881 he had affirmed his position as a naturalist writer, had repeatedly acknowledged his debt to de Coster, had stressed the social duty of the writer, and had insisted that all true art must be conceived in terms of the national temperament. In 1881 he put precept into practice and shocked the bourgeoisie out of their comfortable self-complacency by publishing a novel about which he had been thinking for years and which was destined to remain his masterpiece.[1] *Un Mâle* dealt unashamedly with the sexual lusts and passions of the Belgian peasant, told its story with poetic fervour and rare intensity of feeling, set natural man in all his virility against a wild yet beautiful background of nature, and posed the unresolved conflicts that form the basis of all true tragedy: man against man, against society and its artificial standards of behaviour, against orthodoxy:

[1] Camille Lemonnier wrote, in all, twenty-nine novels and published some twenty volumes of short stories.

Cachaprès était un vrai fils de la terre. Comme l'écorce des
arbres, sa peau rude était durcie au soleil et au gel; il tenait du
chêne par la solitude de ses membres, l'ampleur épanouie de son
torse, la large base de ses pieds fortement attachés au sol . . .
Les gens de la campagne l'aimaient, le sentant avec eux dans
leur révolte basse, leur rancune inavouée contre l'autorité . . .
C'est alors qu'il vit s'épanouir le sourire de Germaine dans un
sourire de mai . . . Il l'aima sans s'en rendre compte, à travers la
neige des étamines, l'aile des papillons, la blancheur du matin,
comme l'incarnation de tout ce qu' il y avait pour lui de désirable
sur la terre, l'ombre des bois, la tiédeur de la plaine, les vergers
pleins de fruits, le meurtre, le vol, la liberté . . . Il avait pour
Germaine l'attachement incoercible de la brute. Il aimait
comme les mâles aiment les femelles.

In Paris the novel was widely acclaimed as an important and
unique contribution to the Naturalist school of writing. In
Belgium sage heads were shaken in disapproval, and when two
years later a jury met to award the *prix quinquennal* for the best
literary effort of recent years it proved too squeamish to award
it to *Un Mâle*. At once Max Waller and his friends were up in
arms, launched a special number of *La Jeune Belgique* in protest,
and organized a banquet in Camille Lemonnier's honour to which
over two hundred guests were invited. The banquet was held on
27 May 1883 and was billed not only in the name of Lemonnier
but also to commemorate Octave Pirmez, who had just died, as
well as all 'unknown heroes' of the country's literature. Georges
Rodenbach spoke for *La Jeune Belgique*. Emile Verhaeren read a
poem in honour of Lemonnier. Edmond Picard, speaking for the
older generation, praised the work of Octave Pirmez, outlined
at length the debt owed to Lemonnier – and then went on to
elaborate his recurrent theme of *l'art social*.

After this demonstration no one could doubt the importance
and influence of *La Jeune Belgique*. By 1886 it was fully grown, its
circulation was continually rising, its ideas were accepted and
circulated by the daily press. It was an institution. But – and
here the cracks were already beginning to appear – it was
dissociating itself from Edmond Picard and even more strenu-
ously from his theory of the social purpose of the artist. *La Jeune
Belgique* stood more intransigently than ever for 'art for art's sake'

and 'le culte de la forme', and its contributors proved more and more intractable to Picard's desire to guide them in the way he thought they should go. They were also offended by his claim that they were in no way unique but rather the fruit of a literary revolution that had been going on for more than twenty-five years. Matters reached a head in the spring of 1885 when Picard, in a rage, physically attacked Albert Giraud, and provoked a duel. Honour was satisfied, no one was hurt, but from then on Picard's own periodical *L'Art Moderne* became increasingly critical of and hostile to *Les Jeunes Belgiques*.

On 18 September 1886, Jean Moréas published in *Le Figaro* his famous article on Symbolism and *La Jeune Belgique* rushed to voice a strong protest against this 'mépris de la langue, la déformation du verbe, une tendance au charabia dont le simple bon sens fait raison'. *La Jeune Belgique*, declared Max Waller, would not follow this example of torturing the French language, but would continue as always to write an impeccable French and to give the Belgian people 'une tradition correcte en même temps qu'artiste'. Picard saw his opportunity, and though he had earlier betrayed misgivings about the Symbolist Movement now veered almost completely in its favour. Verhaeren and Georges Rodenbach, disapproving of Waller's uncompromising attitude, left *La Jeune Belgique* to write for Picard and to open a serious discussion in the pages of *L'Art Moderne* on the work of Mallarmé, Moréas, Verlaine, Gustave Kahn and René Ghil. In this same year also a new literary review, *La Wallonie*, was born, was soon to champion the cause of the Symbolists, and lost no opportunity to taunt *La Jeune Belgique* on its by now reactionary stand and its muddled views on Symbolism.

With the premature and totally unexpected death of Max Waller in 1889 *La Jeune Belgique* lost its real driving force and entered on a final period of slow but inevitable decline. Squabbles between directors and editors allowed for no development of a consistent future line of policy. One by one the poets whom *La Jeune Belgique* had launched left to follow the example of Verhaeren and Rodenbach and to write for either *L'Art Moderne* or *La Wallonie*. Albert Giraud guided the review to a respectable demise on 25 December 1897.

Throughout its sixteen years of existence it had undeviatingly

pursued one aim: that of fostering by all the means in its power
the development of a truly Belgian school of literature based on
uncompromising artistic integrity in thought, feeling and style.
Its honesty and singleness of purpose had made of it a national
institution. It had also brought it enemies. Inescapably it had
become censorious and inflexible – unimaginative even – and
the younger generation, impulsive for change, were heedless of
how revolutionary *La Jeune Belgique* had itself once been. It
endured with a reasonable amount of patience the slights and
taunts of the brash and very young Albert Mockel who con-
trolled the destinies of *La Wallonie*. And it lived on, after all, for
five full years after Mockel's brilliant meteor had burned itself
out. *La Wallonie* was but a springboard. *La Jeune Belgique* was a
platform.

6

Albert MOCKEL (1866–1945) burst like a bombshell on the
University of Liège in October 1884. Ostensibly he was there to
study law. In no time, however, he had gathered around him a
band of eager young men as 'pourris de littérature' as he was
himself, and the bourgeois habitués of café society in Liège soon
had to accustom themselves to the presence amongst them of this
tall, fair-haired, gangling and voluble youth and his retinue of
argumentative and noisy followers. In December 1884, a new
literary society, 'L'Elan', thus came into existence. The following
month Albert Mockel published a mimeographed bulletin,
L'Elan Littéraire, and kept it alive for eighteen months by
printing his own poems and recruiting to his services some of the
best talent available in the university. At this time he was a
fervent admirer of Lemonnier, whom he hailed as 'le héros
national', a doughty champion of the Impressionists in painting,
and a castigator of the city of Liège for her failure to appreciate
the value and importance of her own musicians. He was feeling
his way, and he showed no particular desire to follow the
promptings of certain colleagues and certain other student
reviews to turn *L'Elan Littéraire* into a regional review. Indeed,
he boldly stated that his aim was to encourage all young writers,

remain independent of literary schools, and eschew political discussion of any kind. 'Nous aimons la Wallonie de toutes nos forces; mais . . .'

Towards the middle of 1886 a firm decision was more or less forced on him. A Flemish movement of both political and literary significance had declared itself and that very year a Royal Flemish Academy of Letters had been opened in Ghent. This was a challenge to the supremacy of Walloon culture and of the French tongue that no headstrong and patriotic Liégeois could ignore. Characteristically Mockel decided to sever his connexions with the literary group 'L'Elan' (who were already looking with some misgivings at the expense which the publication of their review put them to) and to found out of his own pocket a new literary review that should stress 'l'étroite parenté de nos provinces demeurées gauloises' and also seek to relate the French culture of Belgium to its central tradition within the culture of France. And whilst Mockel was not politically-minded he did now insist that local literary pride on the part of the Flemings should be matched by a similar pride in the French-speaking provinces of the south. Thus the first number of *La Wallonie* appeared on 15 June 1886, and announced a regional programme with purely artistic aims, frankly progressive in character.

In point of fact it was the progressive tendencies of the review, Mockel's desire always to be ahead of the times, and the deliberate attempt to relate Walloon culture to the French traditional patterns that turned *La Wallonie* into a major literary publication. For the first year of its existence it ambled along cosily enough. Then, in August 1887, Mockel announced that he was opening the pages of *La Wallonie* to French symbolist writers who had been denied a platform through the cessation of publication of their own journal. *La Jeune Belgique* attacked this alliance with Paris. *L'Art Moderne*, originally simply to oppose *La Jeune Belgique*, welcomed the move as one which would strengthen the position of the Symbolist writers in Belgium. This was no more than the truth. From 1887 onwards *La Wallonie* ceased to be provincial in outlook and somewhat esoteric in taste and became the leading Symbolist publication in Europe. Henri de Régnier, Stuart Merrill, Vielé-Griffin, and the 'master'

Mallarmé became contributors. André Gide submitted some
notes on a tour in Britanny in 1891 over the signature of André
Walter, and signed two poems with his own name in 1892. In
1890 Mockel conceived the then novel idea of devoting one
whole number of *La Wallonie* at a time to one given writer, and
the first choice fell on Verhaeren, who was now sending Mockel
most of his output. The beginnings of Symbolist drama were also
heralded by Mockel with the publication in 1889 of Van
Lerberghe's little puppet play *Les Flaireurs,* and in 1890 of
Maeterlinck's *L'Intruse.* With uncanny insight into how Maeterlinck would develop, Mockel tried to explain what these plays
meant in terms of dramatic innovation and argued that the new
Symbolist drama would combine music and poetry to obtain
rhythmic continuity and would seek out legendary subjects to
create the necessary aesthetic distance.

By 1890 Mockel had already settled in Paris at the very hub of
the Symbolist movement, and he was not to return permanently
to his native country until 1937. By 1890 Mockel was convinced
that a triumphant if controversial lecture tour that Mallarmé
made throughout Belgium marked the apotheosis of *La Wallonie.*
The symbolist movement was established and accepted if by no
means fully understood or appreciated. All the young writers
whom he had recruited and publicized were getting ready to
follow their own individual and maturing interests. And Mockel
himself, always impatient to be pushing ahead, had outgrown
the 'little review' stage. He announced a year ahead that *La
Wallonie* would cease publication in 1892, and the last number
proved to be a gigantic 150-page issue of prose and poetry from
the most representative Symbolist writers of France and
Belgium.

Henceforward Mockel devoted himself to perfecting his own
critical techniques, to publishing his own verse, and to making a
thorough study of the whole trend and possibilities of the Symbolist movement. In 1895 he published what still remains the
best critical appreciation of the work of Verhaeren (*Emile Verhaeren, poète de l'énergie*). In 1899 followed his *Stéphane Mallarmé,
un héros.* His own last collection of poems appeared in 1924.
Ultimately, however, his chief claim to recognition lies in his
championing of the Symbolist cause; in providing in *La Wallonie*

a rallying-ground for a group of young men destined to become some of the most important figures in the literary history of Belgium; in his fine critical sense, good taste and sure judgement, and a burning intensity and conviction of purpose which still bears its message to the younger writer of today:

> Viens! Un monde futur tressaille
> et palpite et espère en notre double émoi.

CHAPTER THREE

From Now on (Van Nu En Straks)

I

THE MOVEMENT of the 1880's which produced a flood of minor literary reviews addressed to French-speaking Belgians and that led to the signal achievements of *L'Art Moderne*, *La Jeune Belgique* and *La Wallonie* was naturally matched by a similar movement among the Flemings. Guido Gezelle, for example, had produced and directed his own review as early as 1865. The Flemings, however, steadily conscious of the lead already given them by Henri Conscience and Guido Gezelle, were much more certain of their aims and objectives than were the Walloons, and their approach to developing further the appeal of their native tongue was much influenced by a new literary movement from Holland. This Dutch movement centred on the publication in 1880 of a new review *De Nieuwe Gids* ('The New Guide'), and this review had as its single aim that of raising Dutch literature to the level of other foreign literatures. The members of the movement boldly attacked the pomposity and banality of much of the work of their predecessors, claimed that all true art is compounded of passion and sound common sense, argued that form and content must be one, and extolled the virtues of the 'true' poet who could take the most commonplace subject and give it meaning and significance that transcended its triviality. They were all individualists. In criticism they strove after the most complete objectivity, but in point of fact they were all intensely subjective and lyrical writers.

Flemish writers were quick to sense the importance of this movement and to grasp how they could turn it to their own advantage. They watched its development eagerly, and as eagerly approved. What the Dutch could do for Holland in the field of literature so could they for Dutch-speaking Flanders.

Moreover, both Conscience and Gezelle had shown them the way to go. Their own little reviews in consequence praised Gezelle in particular as the one and 'true' poet for Flanders and urged the implementation of a programme that would not only make Flemish literature a literature in its own right but would also raise the cultural life and standards of the whole Flemish people. One by one these little reviews perished, but their disappearance brought closer together their chief animators and collaborators, and eventually four of these – Auguste Vermeylen, Emmanuel de Bom, Cyriel Buysse and Prosper Van Langendonck – pooled their resources and launched on a prepared public in 1893 their own Flemish counterpart of *De Nieuwe Gids*. They called it *Van Nu En Straks*. Its success was immediate and it is no exaggeration to say that it has influenced the whole trend of Flemish literature down to modern times.

'Van Nu En Straks' is a most difficult expression to translate. Literally, it means 'From Now On', or (as Professor Closset would have it) 'Of Today and Tomorrow'. It is intended to convey an idea of the immediate awakening of the people to their cultural possibilities and to suggest that full realization can only take place in the future. The editors re-affirmed the general policies that the various little reviews had themselves expressed and stressed the fact that in the circumstances they could have no clearly determined artistic principles. Like their Dutch counterparts, they were individualists, but unlike the Dutch they never pushed this to extremes. They were more soberly conscious of the social rôle of the artist, and their deep love for Flanders brought them into much closer contact with the whole way of life of the people whom they sought culturally to emancipate. Between 1893 and 1902 *Van Nu En Straks* provided a platform for almost every possible shade of religious and political opinion. It was avowedly eclectic. All the editors demanded of their contributors was that they should be themselves. 'To be true to yourself', they proclaimed, 'and say exactly where you stand is the only way to uphold the dignity of man. Do not have a purely literary aim in mind, but relate your art to the whole of life.' In other words they were humanists and held firmly to the conviction that work of lasting literary value could only spring from such an approach. Unity must be sought from diversity. Life was itself diversity, and its unifying force hinged on significant moments in the process of evolution. The job of the artist, therefore, was to depict those facets of life he well understood in all their significance, in all their beauty, in their permanence. Once more we are back with Guido Gezelle and the example he himself set as a nature poet, as a religious poet, as one who hymned the beauty and per- manence of God's goodness to man and to nature, and as one who showed how God enhanced man and redeemed him from the sorry perplexities of this life by giving him significance.

2

Auguste VERMEYLEN (1872–1945) soon proved to be the out- standing personality amongst those who launched *Van Nu En Straks*, and he came to hold within the Flemish movement (literary and cultural) a place analogous to that held by André Gide in France or (earlier) by Nietzsche in Germany. He was a critic of remarkable ability and sure judgement and he ex- pressed himself both elegantly and pungently, as the occasion merited. His influence extended not only to the intellectual life of his contemporaries, but also to their literary tastes, to their nationalistic and social convictions, and even to their religious and moral attitudes. His intellectual vigour was phenomenal and he was moved to demand that those who would further the Flemish movement in all its aspects should make a show of 'more brains' (his own expression).

Born in Brussels, he gravitated from the State grammar school to the University of Brussels, studied for a while in Germany where he came under the influence of Hegelian philosophy, taught at the University of Brussels from 1901 until 1923 and became the first rector of the re-constituted and now purely Flemish University of Ghent (1930–1933). His studies of Hegelian philosophy had been expounded to him by a certain Max Stirner who set himself up as the apostle of literary and philosophic anarchism. With Max Stirner he was proud to proclaim: 'I want to be all that I am able to be and to love as much as I am able to love' and he applied this doctrine with remarkable effect in guiding the destinies of *Van Nu En Straks*. Indeed, this

particular brand of anarchism suited his temper perfectly and it
kept his outlook fresh, keen, perceptive and original to the end of
his life.

His first important critical essay, 'Survey of the Flemish
Movement', was published in *Van Nu En Straks* in 1895. In it he
maintains that the Flemish movement, to be properly understood and also to succeed, must be an attempt on the part of the
Flemings to fully develop all their capacities, not only as regards
language but also as regards their cultural and economic life. A
further essay published in 1902 and entitled 'Flemish and the
European Movement' developed these points further and urged
that in order to be a good European a man must first be a good
nationalist. Thus, 'we wish to be Flemings in order to be good
Europeans.' A critical study of Flemish literature from 1830 to
the end of the century was published in 1906, and this was later
completed (1923) by a more detailed survey of the modern
period under the title of *From Gezelle to Timmermans*. The plastic
arts also claimed his attention and in 1921 he published a history
of European painting which, whilst not profound, gave his
readers a clear and synthetic picture of their inheritance.

At a more personal level he wrote many essays and at least two
interesting novels. Here, he tried faithfully to recapture the
crises of incertitude and anxiety through which his own generation had passed, and to give some idea of the idealism that had
fired him and his colleagues, in their youth, to campaign so vigorously for the Flemish movement. His *Wandering Jew*, published
in 1906, showed deep psychological insight and powers of
penetration into character motivation, was written in a clear,
vigorous and compelling style, and became the pattern for
successive generations of Flemish novelists to follow. His *Two
Friends*, first drafted in 1909 but only published in its final form
in 1943, was a moderately successful attempt at depicting the
endless struggle in man to discipline his selfish pursuits and so
give full scope to his natural abilities and talent. The solution
Vermeylen finally propounds is highly characteristic and is a just
measure of his importance to the whole Flemish movement. Life
must be considered as an organic whole. To try to understand
life piecemeal and to live it in fragments is to court disaster. True
quietude of spirit comes from acceptance of the vital rhythm of

life – its *élan vital* – and all true works of art are in harmony with it, isolating neither the individual emotion nor yet the individual standpoint but rather fitting them, with all due emphasis, into the ongoing pattern of development and evolution.

3

The two outstanding novelists of this generation of *Van Nu En Straks*, however, proved to be Cyriel Buysse and Stijn Streuvels (the pen name of Frank Lateur, a nephew of Guido Gezelle). Both set out to depict the life of rural Flanders and both gave the Flemish novel a newer regional approach perhaps not entirely in keeping with Vermeylen's conception of 'europeanization' yet none the less important because of the social issues raised and discussed. They rescued the peasant novel from a state of mediocrity into which the imitators of Henri Conscience had plunged it – Cyriel Buysse by his acute powers of observation and quiet irony, Stijn Streuvels by a kind of brooding lyricism that is often reminiscent of Thomas Hardy in a similar vein.

Cyriel BUYSSE (1859–1932) came of well-to-do Flemish parents, followed the traditional pattern of French education that Maeterlinck had had, was a close friend of Maeterlinck and other authors writing in the French tongue, and took no part at all in the activities of the militant wing of Flemish writers. Indeed, his whole cultural outlook was French and he chose deliberately to write in Flemish because he deplored the scarcity of literary works that the people of Flanders could both want to read and understand. He was much influenced by Zola, and in later life was willing to accept the charge and to admit that Zola's influence had not always been a happy one. Maeterlinck, on the other hand, was quick to recognize him as 'the Flemish Maupassant' and to insist that he was

un Maupassant qui ignore volontairement les villes, les casinos, les grandes dames faisandées, le 'Bel Ami' et les filles. Un Maupassant d'une santé imperturbable et magnifique, un Maupassant exclusivement champêtre qui ne veut s'intéresser qu'aux choses de la vie qui ne passent et ne vieillissent point: le ciel, l'eau, les plaines, les saisons, les villages et les hommes et les femmes qui parlent et pensent encore comme l'eau, les plaines, les arbres et les astres.[1]

We might add that there was also much of Conscience in Buysse: stark realism relieved by a blend of idealism and mysticism and which found its expression in his descriptions of Flanders, his love of nature, and his careful portrayal of the nature of the instinctive attachments of his characters to their native soil. Unlike Conscience, however, who urged the peasantry to accept their lot uncomplainingly and to respect their superiors, Buysse revolted against social injustice of any kind, and with bitter irony castigated the 'little' despots who kept the Flemings in subjection: the chatelain, the notary, the parson, the grocer. All their trickery, deceits, cruelty and lack of humanity are ruthlessly exposed and contrasted with the shocking poverty of the peasantry and the peasantry's moral and intellectual bankruptcy. It is at this point and at this level that, sparing no sordid detail, he most resembles his master, Zola. In many ways also, though he lacks the lyrical compulsion of Camille Lemonnier, Buysse is the Flemish counterpart of his Walloon contemporary.

In all, Buysse wrote some sixty books: novels, plays, collections of short stories and accounts of his travels – all of them carefully recording the lives of the peasantry both rich and poor, of the humble workers and of the bourgeoisie in the small provincial Flemish towns, all telling of their joys and sorrows, their loves and hates, their work and play, and all combining to paint an unforgettable fresco of life in his day in that section of Flanders that stretches between the Scheldt and the river Lys. Perhaps it is in the short story form that he excels, and it is certainly in the title story of one collection of short stories, 'Spring', that he deserves the praise Maeterlinck accorded him. What better Maupassant subject could be found than that of a fashionable young Parisian girl paying her first visit to her three bachelor uncles and spinster aunt living in an isolated farm house in the midst of the Flemish countryside?

With the plays Buysse wrote we shall deal in a later chapter. Of

[1] quoted by Closset: *Aspects et Figures de la littérature flamande*, Brussels, 1944, pp. 58–59

his novels, the most outstanding are *The Right of the Strongest* (1893), *The Life of Rozeke van Dalen* (1905), and *The Little Ball* (1906). *The Right of the Strongest* most forcibly reminds us of Camille Lemonnier's *Un Mâle*. The hero, Balduk, is a superb, dominating figure of a man whose lustful desires the heroine, Maria, in vain seeks to avoid whilst remaining fascinated by his prowess and splendid physique. *The Life of Rozeke van Dalen* deals with the poignant misfortunes befalling a farmer's wife who succumbs to the temptations of another kind of Balduk, and *The Little Ball* traces the story of the degradation and final humiliation of a group of well-to-do villagers.

Stijn STREUVELS (1871–   ) was like Thomas Hardy a country child. His father was a simple tailor and his mother, whose nobility of character and wide knowledge of human nature Streuvels often praises, was obviously the most important influence in his early life. Besides, she was a sister of Guido Gezelle, and was very gifted both in singing and in telling stories. It is customary to claim that Streuvels inherited from his father both his reticent character and his aversion to anything unusual or unexpected. All his life he has certainly shunned the limelight and has tried to allow his early and settled pattern of humdrum existence to prolong itself through to serene and detached old age.

He left school early to be apprenticed to a baker, and in 1887 his parents moved to another village to open their own bakery there. Until the year of his marriage (1905) Stijn Streuvels worked with his parents, read a tremendous amount, and taught himself English, German, French and Norwegian in order to be able to read the recognized best foreign authors in their own tongue. In 1893, so he tells us, the longing to write something himself became overpowering, and he started out, as many another young man has done, with poems and translations. This amiable pursuit, however, failed to satisfy him, and suddenly he began setting down on paper descriptions of his everyday surroundings and accounts of the doings of the country people about him – the peasants, labourers and tradesmen with whom he came into daily contact. With uncanny accuracy he caught the idiom of the people, their changing moods and temper, the drama of their existence. In next to no time Streuvels became a

regular contributor to the leading literary periodicals in both
Flanders and Holland. His masterly command of style won him
immediate respect, and his new 'blend' of realism was exciting.
He could be classified as neither naturalist, nor realist, nor
indeed regionalist. He brought something new that defied
definition, yet possessed an authenticity all its own. He could not
be classified as a pure regionalist, for he spoke for all mankind.
He was more concerned with the total effect of what he wrote, as
a work of art, than with strict adherence to factual detail. And
the life that he depicts, once the alchemy of his own prose style
has worked on a mass of detail, seems much wider and infinitely
more mysterious than can ever be fully grasped through the
senses. Professor Closset sums him up as a 'lyrical realist' and
concludes that

> Streuvels est réaliste avec une pointe de lyrisme. On lui doit une
> peinture des plus fidèles de la vie champêtre flamande au XIXe
> siècle. Streuvels a décrit avec une grande sincérité les passions du
> fragment d'humanité dans lequel il vit chaque jour, celles de
> l'homme fruste, esclave courbé sous la loi inéluctable du travail.
> Il a surtout dit la beauté et la grandeur du paysage de Flandre
> ... La prose de cet auteur impassible est la plus colorée de toute
> la littérature flamande, sa langue dialectale est pittoresque,
> puissante et riche.[1]

In 1899 Streuvels published his first collection of stories under
the somewhat symbolic title of *Lenteleven* ('Spring Life'). Over
the next fifty years he managed to write at least one book a year –
plays, novels, short stories, travel books, memoirs and translations – and he now devotes his old age to a leisurely com-
pilation of his memoirs, four volumes of which have recently
appeared. When he married in 1905, Streuvels left the bakery
to devote himself entirely to literature. He built himself a house –
'The Thrush's Nest' – at Ingooigem in the gently undulating
country to the south of his native West Flanders. All his four
children were born there, and there he has been content to live
and work in close accord with the simple people whom he has
also felt to be his friends.

Streuvels's view of man is unique in Flemish literature in that

[1] Closset: *Aspects et Figures de la littérature flamande*, Brussels, 1944, page 61

he sees him, as did Hardy and Conrad, as governed by a cosmic law. Everything must have its fixed place in the scheme of things and must fulfil its appointed function. In essence, everything is unchangeable, but the outside and casual observer has difficulty in grasping this – in comprehending that whilst humanity is eternal, individual men and women are transient and are granted only a little space in this fixed cosmic order. He who can accept this can get along and find a kind of happiness in his awareness of his unimportance. He who rebels perishes through his rebellion. Thus the heroes of *De Vlaschaard* ('The Flax Field', 1907) and of *De Teleurgang van den Waterboek* ('The Loss of the River Quarter', 1927) are punished with insanity, with mental extinction before their physical death, for having dared oppose the forces of destiny. Even Streuvels's child figures, whom he would have lead an innocently happy life in a daydream world of their own, must sooner or later succumb to their destiny.

For all these reasons Streuvels's heroes are made to work out their fate, not against a conveniently dropped backcloth of nature, but as important and integral elements of the whole forces of nature. They make up a totality with the landscapes they inhabit. It is this preoccupation of Streuvels that leads some critics to accuse him of being repetitious and limited in vision. They forget that he has deliberately limited his art to depict the fortunes of the poor man who must continually drudge away to earn enough to keep alive; that this, too, appears a necessity of nature to Streuvels; and that his workmen are, in consequence, not rebels primarily, but rather marked men who endure their lives with patient resignation. Jan Vandeveughel, the hero of *Langs de Wegen* ('Along the Roads', 1902, and published in English as *Old Jan*) is such a character, and similar characters are equally brilliantly portrayed in minor stories such as *De Oogst* ('The Harvest', 1900), *In 't Water* ('In the Water', 1898), and *De Werkman* ('The Working Man', 1913).

It is in such stories as these, as well as in the masterly *Het Leven en Dood in den Ast* ('Life and Death in the Kiln', 1926), that we get the clearest affirmation of Streuvels's religious beliefs. He believes in God with a peasant's faith. He believes profoundly in mysterious influences that affect people and determine the course of their lives. Nature, therefore, though often wild and

unruly, can never rise up as an enemy against his heroes, as in
Hardy. Nature is never cruel and treacherous, though she may
be indifferent, or seemingly so. It is this simple and direct faith
in God's ultimate goodness that stops Streuvels from being a
depressing author. It is Streuvels's own simplicity of approach
that permits him to catch the bluff, hearty and crude humour of
the peasant types he knows so well and convey its poignancy: it
is the only release from pain and disquiet that they know.

4

Naturally, Buysse and Streuvels had many imitators, but
none was capable of giving the Flemish novel a richer and more
diversified field to cover until Herman TEIRLINCK (1879–)
succeeded in weaning himself from the circumscribing limits
Streuvels's genius had set to novels of rural life and had found the
proper outlet for his own extraordinary powers of evocation, his
dramatic sense, his irony, and his scepticism. Nevertheless, even
in the two novels of rural life with which Teirlinck began his
literary career (*De Wonderbare Wereld* ('The Marvellous World',
1902), and *Het Stille Gesternte* ('The Silent Constellations', 1903)
we can at this distance see that a more subtle and a more complex
and eclectic mind is at work. His approach to the rural novel is
that of the city dweller, and in consequence he sees the countryside more as a curious observer than as a participant, more as an
aesthete, and he mingles not a little fantasy in his observations of
the peasant and the peasant's way of life. Dark and mysterious
forces shape the lives and destinies of his heedless and taciturn
heroes.

From these early beginnings, Teirlinck tentatively shifted his
ironic observations to a series of sketches of the *petite bourgeoisie*,
produced in 1908 his *Mijnheer Serjanszoon*, in 1909 his *Het Ivoren
Aapje* ('The Little Ivory Monkey'), and found himself acclaimed,
somewhat foolishly, as the Anatole France of Flemish letters.
True, the former novel has certain affinities with *La Rôtisserie de
la Reine Pédauque*. The hero is a cultivated Brabançon *rentier*
living in the eighteenth century who discourses wittily on life
and who distils from it, in careful moderation, all the joys and

comforts it has to offer. The latter novel is a bold attempt at depicting and commenting ironically on the teeming and cosmopolitan life of Brussels. Teirlinck, however, despite his smiling scepticism and irony, despite his wealth of imagination and his constant search for the precise and polished word or turn of phrase, lacks the classical purity of style of Anatole France. His artistry is visual. He is more lyrical than meditative in approach. And he is less the detached and amused observer than, as Professor Closset puts it, 'un fantaisiste de la réalité'.

Teirlinck continued cautiously to experiment down to the end of World War I, but the very diversity of his interests and his now recognized eclecticism both prevented a repetition of his early successes and made his readers chary. It is a grave handicap for a young author to be given a label and then for him to set about proving that the wrong label has been attached. In the immediate post-war years he turned his attention and his marked dramatic gifts to achieving a rejuvenation of the Flemish theatre, and then, after this necessarily lengthy period of gestation and preparation, came his masterpiece, *Maria Speermalie* (1940). In this single novel all the diverse talents of Teirlinck are carefully disciplined to tell with dramatic irony and compassion the fortunes of one woman – a kind of Flemish Lady Chatterley – as she progresses from being a lonely orphaned girl through her tentative first love affairs to her betrothal, marriage, and proud position as *châtelaine* of Homveld. The setting is southern Flanders, and the moods of the heroine are matched with the changing seasons and subtly and symbolically linked with a kind of lowering and brooding destiny of purpose that inescapably turns her into a modernized version of Lady Macbeth. It is a haunting and disturbing novel, a novel that once read leaves its mark for ever.

Latterly still more ambitious, Teirlinck has given us his curious epic novel *Het Gevecht met de Engel* ('The Struggle with the Angel', 1952) and his *Zelfportret of het Galgemaal* ('Self-Portrait or Farewell Dinner', 1955). 'The Struggle with the Angel' covers six centuries, and his aim would appear to be to trace the passions of these centuries, one against the other: of landowners against labourers; of nature against civilization; of fathers against sons; of children against themselves; and of primitive

feelings and emotions against middle-class restraint. The title of
the novel itself symbolizes the struggle between discipline and
wildness, and the forest of Soignes, near Brussels, provides the
backcloth against which the whole of the action is measured.
'Self-Portrait' is a novel about a hyper-sensitive old banker
whom Teirlinck follows from youth to old age, tracing every
shameful or hypocritical episode, marking carefully each stage
in the development of his hero, and making the whole uncannily
actual by narrating neither in the first or third person but in a
continuous present in which the principal character is referred
to as 'you'.

5

The one major poet writing in the Flemish tongue who
belongs properly to the generation of *Van Nu En Straks* – and
whose period of creative activity indeed stretches well into
modern times – was Karel van de WOESTIJNE (1878–1929). In a
sense he is both complementary to and yet the direct opposite of
Guido Gezelle; for whilst the latter hymns in simple lyrics the
beauty of Creation, van de Woestijne has almost a pagan conception of life and living, makes articulate the anguish of modern
man, and depicts the haunting and melancholy beauty of city
life. He has himself defined his own poetry as being 'une auto-
biographie devenue symbole', and he attempts to convey to his
reader, not so much by positive affirmation as by a succession of
images that suggest, rather than express, the complexities, the
intensity, and the tragic nature of his own life. In this sense his
work is recognizably cast in the same mould as the tormented
masterpieces of Proust or of D. H. Lawrence. All his art resumes
itself into a struggle between his passionate desire to live and his
fear to act. Bruised by life, wearied in body and soul, he carefully
analyses what he sees, not to describe it with the verve and ironic
detachment of Teirlinck, but rather to distil from it an essential
essence of disillusionment that brings with it none the less some
hope – of what, we know not:

> I am a hazel nut. A pale, soft worm
> lives in my room, and it is blind with greed.

I'm one who feeds on darkness with my seed,
and I become an emptiness that does not speak or heed.

I am outside myself. I suffer from my need.
An endless meal, in a circle closed and firm,
I feed a thankless, dark impatient worm!
But if a child's hand touches me, curious thing:
he hears my hollowness: I sound; I sing!

Van de Woestijne came under the influence of the French symbolists more than any other Flemish writer, and this preoccupation, together with his subtle constructions and turns of phrase and his curious and strange epithets, has made of him a hermetic rather than a popular poet. Neither Baudelaire nor Rilke (van de Woestijne's ultra-refined and sensitive contemporary) has shown himself more deeply personal or more intense. Van de Woestijne's deep introspection is an excuse for self-martyrdom. He is obsessed by sexual desire and the transitory and vain happiness such lust produces. But his obsession is not morbid. He is not so much in love with loving as in expounding the emptiness of such love, in making propitiation for his sin by remorseless self-analysis, in expressing an insatiable yearning for spiritual detachment and repose:

I only ask for rest: I do not ask for peace.
Oh, tender evening-shine of lamps and faces
when noble night rolls up along day's misty places,
when will your pure glow make my worry cease?

I do not ask for peace: I only ask repose,
I only ask the rest that, virgin rose,
comes up like moonrise from the weary day, the mist . . .

Successes at school and at the university left van de Woestijne with no disposition to follow the relatively lucrative family business of coppersmith. He took to writing straight away and earned his living in the early days by becoming a correspondent and literary critic of one of the leading Dutch newspapers. Then, as his reputation and position as the leading intellectual and Flemish man of letters of his day became assured, he was appointed professor of Flemish literature in the University of Ghent, his native town. It was there that he finally succumbed to pulmonary tuberculosis.

His first collection of verse, *Het Vaderhuis* ('The Family Home') appeared in 1903 and traced the life of the sensitive youth down to his first tentative love affairs. In 1905 he published *De Boomgaard der Vogelen en Fruchten* ('The Orchard of Birds and Fruits') in which he told of his engagement and early married life in the valley of the Lys. There followed in 1910 *De Gulden Schaduw* ('The Golden Shadow') which hymned the joys of paternity, the blessing of family life and the beauties of nature. In 1920 came the final autobiographical volume, *De Modderen Man* ('Man of Clay'), which traces advancing age, regrets all unrealized dreams and aspirations and speaks poignantly of the awakening of new and unsatisfied desires. In 1910 and in 1920 he published three volumes of epic poetry, later grouped into two volumes with the title of *Interludes* (1924–1926). To *De Modderen Man* he later added *God aan Zee* ('God at the Seaside') and *Het Bergmeer* ('The Mountain Lake') to make up the trilogy entitled *Wiekslag om de Kim* ('Winging over the Horizon', 1928).

The prose writings and literary criticism of van de Woestijne have about them the same striking allusiveness as his poetry, the same hermetic style, the same preoccupations, and it is here above all that he shows himself an apt disciple of Vermeylen, though as an unsatiated seeker after beauty and truth he does not aim at the synthesis of art and life so dear to Vermeylen. All van de Woestijne's writing, indeed, has a strange heavy music of its own. His themes are few, repeated and mannered. But he brought a richness of tone and mood that was new in Flemish literature. For all these reasons he has never been a popular writer, and he would have considered popularity in a sense a prostitution of his genius. For all these reasons also he can lay just claim, along with Vermeylen and Teirlinck, to being instrumental in bringing Flemish literature out of its provincial phase to give it both stature and dignity.

6

So ended the first phase of what we might term the moderniz-
ation of the Flemish literary movement. The writers who had
grouped themselves around *Van Nu En Straks* were fervent
admirers of the folklore, customs and culture of their native
Flanders and sought to extol all the virtues they found there.
This led them, in most instances, to be particularist in their
approach in that they betrayed a tender devotion to their own
native province, city or village. This narrowing of the view led in
turn to a most careful documentation and to the most scrupulous
honesty in depicting human nature, human weaknesses and
human foibles. Yet they could not be called either realist or
naturalistic writers. Their almost apostolic fervour for Flanders
had about it a persuasive clarion call that was matched only,
perhaps, by Walt Whitman's championing of the New World.

Again, their own particular brand of realism and their extraordinary descriptive sense had about it either the mystical
exactitude of the Van Eyck brothers or the fleshy contours of
Rubens. True, many of them were deeply influenced by
Scandinavian and Russian literature (particularly Dostoievsky)
and by Emile Zola, but their predilection for these writers was
matched by their own feelings of unease and incertitude, by
feelings of pity and despair before the incomprehensible mystery
of creation, by a kind tortured sympathy for the lot of man. Such
realism as theirs is not limited to the visible. Death is always
present, the supernatural much in evidence. Philosophically
speaking, they are determinists. And all, consciously or unconsciously, responded nobly to the challenge of 'europeanization' that Vermeylen set them.

Four Symbolist Poets

I

ONE OF the most interesting consequences of Albert Mockel's decision to open the pages of *La Wallonie* to the dispossessed French symbolist writers was to make plain the essential differences between the French and Belgian concept of symbolism as such. For if in France the symbolist movement became an aristocratic and anti-bourgeois movement, a revolt against realism in art and the coldly chiselled perfection of the *Ecole Parnasse*, an artistic protest against the dull drabness of the Third Republic, it was in Belgium something much more vital, much more 'native'. There was neither need nor call for a revolt on the part of the Belgian writers. That most individual and most robust of the Belgian symbolist writers, Emile Verhaeren, once defined symbolism as any work of art, not being allegory or myth, whose evident purpose is to express the artistic attitude; and in speaking thus he was defining the attitude of the Belgian people towards artistic creation, not only in the actual and present, but down through the ages. In other words, the Belgians, and particularly the Flemings, have always had a strong vein of mysticism running through their entire approach to life and living, and they have in consequence almost unconsciously cultivated the aesthetic symbol. Without this the work of the Flemish primitives could not now delight us; without it we should not have had *L'Agneau Mystique*; without it we should not have had the literary revival in Belgium based on folklore, legend and popular song; without it the particular genius of Maeterlinck (whom we shall discuss in a separate chapter) and of Verhaeren, Van Lerberghe, Grégoire Le Roy and Max Elskamp could not so decisively have asserted itself.

It is to be noted once again that all these writers were Flemings

educated in the French tradition and that all but Elskamp were
at the same Jesuit college of Sainte-Barbe in Ghent. Yet though
they were friends they could in no sense be described as a coterie.
Like all true Belgians they were individualists. They differed
from the French symbolists in that again, like all Belgians, they
refused to be circumscribed even by self-imposed rules and so
could never observe so complete a break with the Parnassian
movement as their French counterparts. They were not interested
in theories as such. They knew, intuitively, that the external
world is not important and that it can have no meaning until the
artist has seen it significantly. Baudelaire's theory of earthly
correspondances meant little to them. They were personally (as
opposed to academically) involved in the mystery of being.
Symbolism for them was a means to an end and not an end in
itself. It was a liberating force that enabled them to realize
themselves to the full. And so it was that Charles Van Lerberghe
could write:

> Ce que je recherche exclusivement c'est la Beauté, et encore une
> certaine beauté à la grecque, je veux dire qui peut sembler in-
> expressible et froide. . . . La Beauté à mes yeux est aussi toujours
> plus ou moins voilée . . . Et parmi les règles d'art que j'ai tou-
> jours observées, il y a celle d'E. Poe reprise par Baudelaire . . .
> qu'il n'y a pas de beauté sans une certaine étrangeté.

Or, as the distinguished Belgian critic, Paul Hamélius, has
reminded us, Belgian writers of the symbolist movement all
aimed at a poetic form of expression in which subject matter and
imagery should fuse and dissolve to lose their separate meanings
the better to convey the central idea.[1] Once more we are back
among the Flemish primitives and in the presence of the incomparable *Agneau Mystique*.

2

Emile VERHAEREN (1855–1916) perhaps best illustrates those
differences between French and Belgian symbolist poets I have
been trying to describe. From the beginning he was determined

[1] *La Littérature française et flamande de Belgique*, Brussels, 1921, pp. 271–278

to identify himself with the deep instincts of his native Flanders. All his career is one long effort towards achieving new thoughts and new forms of expression. His attitude to life is thus unlike that of Mallarmé or Verlaine. He is optimistically attracted to existence. He is passionately interested in its concrete variety, in the forms and appearances of nature and in human reactions to them, in all the tragic and joyous aspects of life. He develops an acute sense of the poetry of modern civilization, and his verse vibrates in unison with the cares and hopes of *his* people and *his* age. He sings life exuberant. And he sees all with the sure eye of the painter:

> Une place minime et quelques rues
> Avec un Christ au carrefour;
> Et l'Escaut gris avec sa tour
> Qui se mire parmi les eaux bourrues.

Such is the description he gives us, in a few bold and telling strokes, of his birthplace, Saint-Amand. He was the son of well-to-do and pious bourgeois parents and his education followed the routine pattern: the fashionable Jesuit college in Ghent, the Catholic University of Louvain to study law, and then chambers in Brussels – with Edmond Picard. On his own admission he was an indifferent and uninterested pupil, taking much more pleasure in frequenting painters and writers of the day through his renewed friendship with Georges Rodenbach than in caring for the affairs of his clients. He had already published poems – mainly imitative of Lamartine and Hugo – in a student magazine he had edited at Louvain. His arrival in Brussels (1881) coincided with the founding of *L'Art Moderne* and *La Jeune Belgique*, and the inspiration and encouragement he drew from now living among men who cared passionately and deeply for the arts led to the publication in 1883 of his first collected volume of verse, *Les Flamandes*.

Encouraged by Edmond Picard, he now abandoned law and set about preparing himself for his true vocation as a poet by embarking with three artist companions on a lengthy period of travel which took him to Spain, London (whence came the inspiration for *Les Villes Tentaculaires*), Paris and Berlin. He returned feverishly excited by his experiences, filled with exuberance for the spectacle modern man presented, freed from the narrow provincialism of his upbringing, yet at the same time a prey to moral and religious doubts and remorse. A retreat to a Cistercian monastery staved off a threatened nervous breakdown and gave him the material for his second volume of verse, *Les Moines* (1886) – sensuous poems that accurately depicted life in a Flemish monastery and endowed the monks with an asceticism as savage and as voluptuous as the joyousness of living illustrated in *Les Flamandes*.

The death of his parents in 1888, however, increased his gloom and despair, and there then followed in rapid succession *Les Soirs* (1888), *Les Débâcles* (1889), and *Les Flambeaux Noirs* (1891), aptly described by Albert Mockel as 'une trilogie de la souffrance'. In suffering the poet matured and prepared for himself reserves for his final and greatest period. A happy marriage in 1891, the keen interest he began to take in social problems, and the genuine interest with which his work was at last being acclaimed finally saved him from himself. A busy routine and round of activities added purpose and balance to his existence. He spent the winter months in Paris, the spring in his beloved country retreat in the province of Hainaut, the summer at Westende on the Belgian coast to care for his persistent attacks of hay fever. He interested himself with Eekhoud and the Socialist leader Vandervelde in the *Maison du Peuple* in Brussels. He travelled throughout Europe.

His two first books had revealed him as a realist with the painter's sure eye for the telling detail, who was working very much in the Parnassian tradition. The 'trilogy of suffering' had sombre symbolist undertones. He now published in rapid succession *Les Campagnes Hallucinées* (1893), in which he describes the desolation of the countryside that has been deserted to glut the cities; *Les Villages Illusoires* (1895), which is all symbolism, the ferryman being the stubborn artist who holds the green reed of hope between his teeth, the fishermen symbolizing the selfish society of the day, and the rope-maker weaving the horizons of the future; *Les Villes Tentaculaires* (1895), which gives a clear cinematographic picture of a town – any town, though London is at the back of the poet's mind. And this second trilogy is one in which contemporary life is reviewed, reviled, condoned, explained and finally reconciled with beauty – a beauty owing nothing to the Grecian ideal, but a beauty that is not to be seen in the outward form but in the idea that gives that outward form its power, its energy, its finality.

The publication of *Les Heures Claires* (1896) was a sincere and moving tribute to his wife for the serenity and balance of mind he had by now achieved. And then came a tumbling, rushing paean of praise in favour of modern man and the modern machine age that should make all things possible:

> O ce travail farouche, âpre, tenace, austère,
> Sur les plaines, parmi les mers, au cœur des monts,
> Serrant ses nœuds partout et rivant ses chaînons
> De l'un à l'autre bout des pays de la terre!
> O ces gestes hardis, dans l'ombre ou la clarté,
> Ces bras toujours ardents et ces mains jamais lasses,
> Ces bras, ces mains unis à travers les espaces
> Pour imprimer quand même à l'univers dompté
> La marque de l'étreinte et de la force humaines
> Et recréer les monts et les mers et les plaines,
>   D'après une autre volonté.

Les Visages de la Vie (1899), *Les Forces Tumultueuses* (1902), *La Multiple Splendeur* (1906), *Les Rhythmes Souverains* (1910) – all won him acclaim and a still wider reading public. He was hailed as the European Walt Whitman (whom he much admired), as 'le grand barbare du nord', as the true interpreter of the magnificent effort of man and of the joy man experiences in creating and conquering, as the prophet of fraternity who sang the tender and tremendous joy of living.

Yet all this febrile expenditure of energy depended on two things: his stable married life and his recollections of a happy childhood in his beloved Flemish province. Again and again he returns in his thoughts and writings to the Flanders of his youth, yearns for the innocence and pleasures that were his, uncannily catches the passing mood and moment, calms and consoles himself with the security and release marriage has brought him:

> C'est la bonne heure où la lampe s'allume,
>   Où les aveux

De s'être aimés le jour durant,
Du fond du cœur profond mais transparent,
    S'exhument.

    Et l'on se dit les simples choses:
Le fruit qu'on a cueilli dans le jardin;
    La fleur qui s'est ouverte,
    D'entre les mousses vertes;

Et la pensée éclose, en des émois soudains,
    Au souvenir d'un mot de tendresse fanée
        Surpris au fond d'un vieux tiroir,
            Sur un billet de l'autre année.

Between 1904 and 1911 he published five separate collections of verse under the general title of *Toute la Flandre,* in which he attempted faithfully to portray all the sensual delight and pleasure he took in the changing panorama he caused to unfold itself before his readers. Of his earliest youth he writes:

Je me souviens de la bonne saison;
Des parlottes, l'été, au seuil de la maison
Et du jardin plein de lumière,
Avec des fleurs, devant, et des étangs, derrière;
Je me souviens des plus hauts peupliers,
De la volière et de la vigne en espalier
Et des oiseaux, pareils à des flammes solaires.

Of the bargee:

    Sur l'arrière de son bateau
    Le batelier promène
    Sa maison naine
    Par les canaux.

    Elle est joyeuse, et nette, et lisse,
    Et glisse
    Tranquillement sur le chemin des eaux.
    Cloisons rouges et porte verte,
    Et frais et blancs rideaux
    Aux fenêtres ouvertes.

C

Of the dune-swept coast in the heat of the summer sun:

> Et midi luit comme un glaive
> La mer lasse ne peigne plus
> Ses flots bouffants et chevelus
> Au long des grèves.

Bruegel-like, of the Shrove Tuesday village junketing:

> Jour de fête, jour de bien-être!
> On regarde, par les fenêtres,
> Hommes, femmes, enfants et vieux
> Couper les pains par le milieu
> Et tout à coup, crever le boudin formidable.
> Lards et graisses poissent la table.
> Du lait crémeux, du café chaud
> Emplit jusques au bord les pots,
> Et dans un coin les chiens grognent et se querellent
> Autour des croûtes et des peaux
> Qu'on leur jette au hasard en de larges écuelles . . .

And, finally, a sincere tribute to the true source of all his inspiration:

> Les plus belles idées
> Qui réchauffent mon front
> Tu me les a données . . .
> Escaut! Escaut!
> Tu es le geste clair
> Que la patrie entière
> Pour gagner l'infini fait vers la mer.

The happiness of his last years was clouded by the outbreak of World War I, which effectively put an end to all his dreams and aspirations for modern man. He stoically placed his talents at the service of his country, toured and lectured, published a last volume of patriotic verse, *Les Ailes Rouges de la Guerre* (1916), and then – falling victim to a stupid accident – was run over and killed by a train in the station of Rouen. Characteristically, his last words were: 'Ma patrie! . . . Ma femme!'

Albert Mockel, though full of praise for the work of Verhaeren, was at the same time highly critical of his faults. He claimed that

Verhaeren was too much the poet and too little the artist; that he was a romantic with the old looseness, eloquence and panache; that he was also too modern and forbidding in his modernity. 'One does not like Verhaeren's poems,' he wrote, 'one accepts them.' Admittedly, Verhaeren, like Hugo, wrote too much – thirty published volumes in all, and four plays – and like Hugo he has since suffered an unmerited eclipse. None the less, he is the greatest of the Belgian poets and the most modern of the poets of his generation. He has the sweep, the vigour and the direct frankness of Walt Whitman, and he uses the symbolist technique to forge for himself a form of verse dictated solely by the emotional necessity for conveying vividly to the reader the urgency of his message. He is the first writer, after De Coster, to address himself directly to the Belgian people and to impose a purely Belgian way of thinking, feeling and speaking for the people. Nor should we forget that whilst Whitman was hymning with nationalistic fervour the importance of the modern American concept of life and living, and whilst Nietzsche was formulating his doctrine of the Superman, Verhaeren was seeking the brotherhood of all men and trying to put over his message that modern technical progress and development, rightly used, was the potent instrument to that end.

Again, the comparison with Hugo and the link with the romantics, though perhaps inevitable, is none the less unjust. He was much more clearly the prophet and seer than was Hugo. Hugo postured. Verhaeren saw clearly and believed sincerely and passionately in what he saw. Nor could Hugo, for all his poetic genius, match Verhaeren's skill in capturing all the varied moods of nature. As one critic puts it, 'Nul n'a su comme lui ... exprimer avec cette énergie terrible la puissance des éléments déchaînés':

> Sur la bruyère longue infiniment,
> Voici le vent cornant novembre,
> Sur la bruyère, infiniment,
> Voici le vent
> Qui se déchire et se démembre,
> En souffles lourds battant les bourgs,
> Voici le vent,
> Le vent sauvage de novembre.

In effect, Verhaeren brings a new sensitivity and feeling tone to
the poetry of his day, and the powerful originality of his inspiration and his means of expression set him distinctly apart
from either the romantics, or the *Ecole Parnasse*, or the Symbolists.
When he was at the height of his popularity it was felt that a new
Belgian school of symbolist writers was in process of being
created. Such proved not to be the case. He has had only pale
and mediocre imitators. And that is the best testimonial that
stands to his genius.

3

Charles VAN LERBERGHE (1861–1907) presents a complete
contrast to Verhaeren, lacks his exuberance and care for all
things Flemish, and, if it be accepted that Verhaeren was much
more of a poet than an artist, then he, Van Lerberghe, was much
more the artist than the poet. His is what has come to be described
as 'pure' poetry: it is limpid, musical, polished; it is, as he would
have it be, 'l'éternelle chanson de l'âme humaine'; it lacks the
mysterious, evocative background of Maeterlinck, and is all
innocence and peace – emotion recollected in tranquillity:

> Une voix divine a chanté
> En son mystérieux langage
> Le doux songe de la beauté
> A travers de pâles images.

He was a somewhat solitary and introspective child, saddened
first by the loss of his father when he himself was only seven, then
by a serious illness when he was only thirteen, and finally by the
death of his mother when he was barely recovered. Fortunately,
he and his sister were well provided for, and his guardian was
none other than Maeterlinck's uncle who first sent the ailing boy
to the country to build him up and then packed him off to the
Collège Sainte-Barbe where he found himself in the same classes
as the young Maeterlinck and Grégoire Le Roy. He lived with
his sister in one of the most picturesque parts of Ghent, near the
old *béguinage*, and from there was early writing sonnets which

attracted the admiration of Rodenbach who summed him up even at this early date as 'le poète de la résignation'. With Maeterlinck and Le Roy he studied literature at the University of Ghent; with them he helped to found a French literary review, *La Pléiade*, in which his first printed verse appeared (1886); with them he went to Paris, met Verhaeren, and under the friendly tutelage of Rodenbach was quietly launched as a promising young poet. Already, he was much under the influence of Maeterlinck, and like him (and Verhaeren) was already turning himself into a serious student of art.

The first poems of these three friends to appear in Belgium were published in *La Jeune Belgique*, but all three were quickly attracted to Albert Mockel's meteoric *La Wallonie* after his enthusiastic and sincere praise of their work in the former review. To Van Lerberghe fell the distinction of creating symbolist drama by the publication of his play, *Les Flaireuses*, in the pages of *La Wallonie* in January 1889. A year later (in January 1890) Maeterlinck gave Mockel a play on a closely similar theme called *L'Intruse*. Immediately the critics were attacking the lesser-known Van Lerberghe for plagiarism, so much so that when Van Lerberghe's play was finally produced in Paris in 1892, Maeterlinck felt impelled to include a note in the programme to inform the public that

> *Les Flaireuses* ne ressemblent pas à *L'Intruse*, mais *L'Intruse* ressemble aux *Flaireuses*, et elle est fille de ceux-ci. Au reste, si le thème des deux drames est à peu près identique, on verra qu'il y a, ici, une puissance de symbolisation qu'on ne retrouve pas dans ma petite pièce . . .

It was a generous gesture, for there can be no doubt that whilst there are many affinities between the two plays, Maeterlinck's *L'Intruse* is the more accomplished and artistically satisfying. It would seem that Van Lerberghe needed to write this play of his in order to purge himself of all the dark and brooding thoughts that prevented him from achieving that tranquillity and detachment of mind which his major work demanded. For *Les Flaireuses* is not so much a tragedy as a macabre recital of the gruesome. The influence of Ibsen is obvious and he claims to have been inspired by his reading of Edgar Allan Poe (*The Raven*), and by Dürer, Holbein and Bruegel. Van Lerberghe has given us a kind of mystery play in three parts, based on a theme very common in Flemish and German literature of the Middle Ages: the horror of a young girl confronted with death. There is no plot, and the three emissaries that Death sends to the house of the girl to announce to her the inevitable and inescapable combine with a variety of stage effects – flickering candles, a funeral march, the shadow of a hearse, etc. – to achieve an extraordinary dramatic tension.

By 1890 Van Lerberghe had settled in Brussels, and for the next few years he led a quiet, peaceful existence, reading and translating from the English, taking his doctorate at the university (1894), writing critical essays on the work of his friends, Maeterlinck and Grégoire Le Roy, contributing a handful of delightful prose-poems to *La Wallonie*, and slowly preparing – with much encouragement from Maeterlinck and Fernand Séverin – his first collection of poems. This appeared in 1898 with the title of *Entrevisions* and won him immediate praise from a small and select group of discerning critics. The influence of his studies of the Flemish primitives and of his enthusiasm for the pre-Raphaelites is immediately obvious. There is a subtle marriage of pagan symbol with Christian myth. The theme is simple yet difficult to pinpoint. As Rémy de Gourmont remarked, 'Ce sont-là des aspects fugitifs et changeants, des images à peine dessinées, des demi-souvenirs.' The poet glimpses how beauty and goodness encompass us with 'des cercles dont nous ne sortirons pas'; divines how joy is compounded of the simplest of things; hymns the soul's dream-like quest of the eternally unattainable; in a quiet ecstasy of mind accepts the assurance that

Un jour nouveau se lève dans la splendeur du monde.

The urge to travel now visited him again. He came to London and was captivated by the poetry of William Butler Yeats. He abandoned Brussels for a delightful country retreat near Bouillon and there began to plan what was to be his masterpiece, *Chanson d'Eve*. To Fernand Séverin he outlined what he had in mind:

Aube du Paradis. Paysage où rien ne se distingue encore, sorte de fleur immense et confuse qui s'ouvre lentement (facile à dire, mais, pour l'écrire, je ne connais jusqu'ici que Mallarmé dans le début de *L'Après-Midi d'un Faune*, qui ait su donner une pareille impression).

From Bouillon he left on a two-year journey that took him to Berlin, to Munich, and finally through Italy to Rome, Florence and Venice. It was in Florence, in the garden of *Torre del Gallo*, on a hill overlooking the city, that most of *Chanson d'Eve* took shape. He was to write later:

Tous mes poèmes sont des tableaux. Ma *Chanson d'Eve* est peinte autant que chantée. J'allais passer des heures, le matin, des heures d'adoration ravie devant la naissance de Vénus de Botticelli ou l'Annonciation de Léonard, et je rentrais dans mon jardin les yeux remplis de cet éblouissement.

He returned to Belgium in 1901, obtained an appointment at the Musée Royal des Arts Décoratifs, and tried to resolve a love affair with a young Italian girl who had followed him back home. Too timid, too scrupulous, too introspective, he could not bring himself to marry the girl and he quickly gave up his museum appointment to retire once again to Bouillon and to spend the next two years polishing and re-polishing his *Chanson d'Eve* under the critical eye and friendly guidance of Mallarmé. The poem finally appeared in 1904. Praise for the work was fulsome and immediate but, as with *Entrevisions*, came only from among a small group of people sensitive to the poet's intention.

Chanson d'Eve is divided into five separate parts: 'Prélude', 'Premières Paroles', 'La Tentation', 'La Faute', and 'Le Crépuscule'. The aim is to evoke Eve, the symbol of all womanhood, from the dawn of innocence:

> Dans un parfum de roses blanches
> Elle est assise et songe;
> Et l'ombre est belle comme s'il s'y mirait un ange.

to her awakening to life and love:

Et je revis auprès de l'Arbre merveilleux
Le jeune dieu aux cheveux d'hyacinthe,
De roses couronné.
Ses regards, qui suivaient l'amoureuse descente
D'une étoile, s'étaient avec elle inclinés
Vers la terre. Ses lèvres souriaient.

to the Fall:

Eve pleurait. Ses mains cachaient sa tête pâle.
C'était le premier soir mortel.
Des êtres lumineux descendirent du ciel,
Et l'air s'emplit du chant de leur voix amicale.

to the final renunciation of Paradise:

L'âme chantante d'Eve expire,
Elle s'éteint dans la clarté;
Elle retourne en un sourire
A l'univers qu'elle a chanté . . .

En de vagues accords où se mêlent
Des battements d'ailes,
Des sons d'étoiles,
Des chutes de fleurs,
En l'universelle rumeur
Elle se fond, doucement, et s'achève,
La chanson d'Eve.

The only other major work Van Lerberghe produced was a play, *Pan* (1906), at which he had worked in his country retreat whilst revising *Chanson d'Eve*. He claimed that he was inspired by the fantasy element he found in the paintings of Bruegel. Pan comes back to life in a shepherd's hut somewhere in Flanders, claims a ready following from amongst the poor and simple of heart, but is bitterly attacked by the established order as represented by a burgomaster who at all costs wishes to avoid trouble, and by an abbot zealous in his pursuit of the devil. The only person open to new ideas is a teacher! It is a satirical play, a farce in the grand, comic style of the middle ages, a play of grotesques – and it should be judged as such. Unfortunately, because of its marked anti-clerical tendencies, it not only met with an undeservedly cool reception but also succeeded in alienating his family from him. A year later Van Lerberghe had died of a cerebral haemorrhage, having fallen ill some months previously whilst on a visit to Grégoire Le Roy.

Compared with Verhaeren and Maeterlinck his output was small: two volumes of verse, two plays, and a handful of essays and prose-poems. He had neither the robust energy of speech of Verhaeren nor Verhaeren's desire to speak to and for the people; he was no visionary in Verhaeren's sense nor could he glorify the present. Similarly, he lacked Maeterlinck's broad intellectual sweep and range of power. His was a withdrawn and introspective nature, passionately questing beauty and at the same time disciplining itself most severely to accept only the quintessence: that which lay beyond the material world of earth, water, fire and air. The broad, Bruegel-like sweeps of Verhaeren he ignored in order to see beyond what Bruegel portrayed; he made Maeterlinck's tentative poetic efforts in the same direction seem juvenile in comparison. In short, he added to French verse what it had so far missed: a very precise appeal to the unprecise that Nerval, Mallarmé and Paul Valéry in turn strove unsuccessfully, by the standards he set, to accomplish.

4

Grégoire LE ROY (1862–1941) can be represented as standing midway between the two extreme positions maintained by Verhaeren and Van Lerberghe. He is fascinated by the tempo of modern life, yet he yearns nostalgically for the past in proportion as he grows uneasy about the present. Sadness and a kind of numb despair at the greyness of life permeate all his work:

> Le corps se meurt par les années
> Et l'âme se meurt par l'oubli.

Like Verhaeren, he harks back to his childhood days and vividly recaptures the scene in his father's workshop where poor but pious women 'alanguissaient les après-midi par des cantiques chantés en chœur et attristaient les soirs par le bourdonnement des prières récitées à haute voix.' Like Verhaeren he sings of and for the people, but it is a plaintive song sympathizing with their poverty and unfulfilled dreams:

> La vieille file et son rouet
> Parle de vieilles, vieilles choses;
> La vieille a les paupières closes
> Et croit bercer son vieux jouet.

Like Verhaeren he has the painter's eye and the sure touch for fixing an animated small-town scene:

> Roucoulements très doux, très lents,
> Et plaintes de moutons bêlants,
> Et chants de coq et cris de poule,
> Et voix de peuple qui se saoule;
>
> Au haut des toits des paons chantant
> Des pleurs d'enfants que l'on entend,
> Et cris de mère qui les gronde
> Là-bas, dans une cour immonde.

But the gusto and zest of Verhaeren is lacking, and the verve of Verhaeren is replaced by a meticulous artistry of composition that recalls the best of Van Lerberghe and finally sweeps us away to regions that only Van Lerberghe and Grégoire Le Roy could explore:

> Il pleut si misérablement
> Sur ma barque et dans l'eau qui pleure!
> Il pleut des lames sur la terre,
> Et puis c'est l'heure,
> Et c'est l'universel mystère,
> Et puis il pleut si tristement
> Sur ma barque et dans l'eau qui pleure!
>
> Viens dans ma barque de misère!
> Nous voguerons sur l'eau qui pleure...
> Nous irons au lac de mystère
> Où s'entend la voix éperdue

D'une princesse légendaire
Qui pleure là, qui pleure
La barque à tout jamais perdue
Au fond des eaux
Dans les roseaux.

In Paris, Grégoire Le Roy threw himself much more vigorously into his art studies than did either of his two friends, Maeterlinck and Van Lerberghe. He took painting lessons in studios of approved artists and studied anatomy at the Ecole des Beaux Arts. He was content, however, to return to Ghent in the winter of 1886–87 with Van Lerberghe and to lead a placid, provincial existence during which time he prepared his first collection of poems, *La Chanson du Soir*, which he published privately in a small limited edition of twenty copies. In 1889 came a second collection, *Mon Cœur pleure d'autrefois*, and then, tiring of 'an artist's inactivity', he took himself away to Brussels and became a small business tycoon in the newly booming electrical trade! This curious enterprise ended with the publication in 1907 of his collected works along with a new piece, *La Chanson du Pauvre*, which gave the book its title. From 1909 to 1919 he was librarian to the Brussels Académie des Beaux-Arts, and from 1919 until two years before his death he remained keeper of the Musée Wiertz. Apart from two collections of short stories and an excellent monograph on the painter, James Ensor, he gave us during this last uneventful period of his life three further volumes of poetry: *La Couronne des Soirs* (1912), *Les Chemins dans l'Ombre* (1920), and *L'Ombre sur la Ville* (1935).

More Parnassian than symbolist in his conception of the function of poetry, he none the less consistently strives for that obliquity of symbol and image that all true Symbolists like Van Lerberghe felt necessary if the emotions awakened by the constant and patient search for the unattainable were to be truly mirrored. He is not a pure poet in that he cannot sufficiently disengage himself from preoccupation with his immediate environment. And because he cannot accept his environment as did Verhaeren, nor soar above it as did Van Lerberghe, the quality of his writing inevitably suffers. On the other hand, at his best he succeeds in matching the rhythms of popular song to the hopes and aspirations of the poor and humble, and his *La Chanson du Pauvre* – by far his best work – has a true and authentic note.

5

Max ELSKAMP (1862–1931) is the one truly Catholic poet in this group of Symbolist writers, and in his more robust and optimistic moods his work has striking affinities with that of Francis Jammes. In all other respects, however, he was the 'outsider'. All his life he shrank from allowing his poems to reach even a select reading public. A wood engraver of real talent and ability, he illustrated his own works and then issued them in small editions reserved usually only for his friends; and he left instructions that posthumous collections of his work should be the sole property of certain recognized public libraries. He at no time doubted his own genius, but he preferred to keep contact with his own intimate thoughts, feelings and aspirations for those who might fully understand what he was about. He is in every respect a folklore poet, often deliberately using an archaic form of language, often twisting the syntax the better to serve his own deeper purpose and achieve his effect, yet wedding the whole to a simple, popular rhythm:

> J'ai triste de mon cœur en bois,
> Et j'ai très triste de mes pierres,
> Et des maisons où, dans du froid,
> Au dimanche des cœurs de bois,
> Les lampes mangent la lumière.

Again, the folklore or popular type of poem is often abandoned for a litany or a kind of plainsong of haunting and poignant simplicity:

> Dans la misère qu'on a eue,
> Dans la peine qu'on a portée,
>
> C'est toutes choses accomplies
> Et sur les doigts qu'on a comptées,

Ames ici qui se délient,
Amères et de réfugiés.

As one critic has put it, he has 'une âme ingénue de primitif, une
sensibilité attendrie et pieuse, une inspiration rêveuse et calme'.
Again and again he elaborates three or four simple themes
remembered from his childhood spent on a bustling and
picturesque stretch of the river Scheldt, in Antwerp, in the old
part of the town near the Eglise Saint-Paul: smiling madonnas
at each street corner; crucifixes, calvaries, religious processions;
the bustling life of the ships in port, telling the past and present
glories of the town; the homely customs and habits of the poor
and simple of heart.

His father was a rich banker and business man, and for the
first eight years of his life Max Elskamp roamed the streets of his
native quarter of the town, beguiled by the mystery of it all,
deeply impressed by the quiet and peace of the ancient *béguinage*
of the Rue Rouge, moved to tears by Rubens' picture of 'The
Flagellation' in a nearby Dominican church. When his sister
Maria was born the family moved to the more fashionable
Boulevard Léopold and Max entered the local *Athénée* (grammar
school) to begin his studies. From there he went to study law at
the University of Brussels, returned to Antwerp formally to
register himself as a barrister – though he never pleaded – and
then set out on a three-year journey (1884–1887) which took him
to Germany, Italy, Switzerland, France and Spain. He was an
accomplished fencer, oarsman and yachtsman, and he never
again left Antwerp, finding that this stretch of the Belgian coast
offered him all he asked for and that people were more than
ready to come and see him rather than put him to the trouble of
visiting them. So it was that he met Albert Mockel and gave him
in 1891 two rather laboured prose-poems for *La Wallonie* and
three poems from his *Salutations, dont d'Angéliques* (1893). Later,
he was to take sailing on the Scheldt, though on different
occasions, both Mallarmé and Verlaine.

Slim volumes of verse appeared at regular intervals between
1892 and 1896 to be collected together as *La Louange de la Vie*
(1898), in which latter year he also published *Enluminures*. Then
a long silence, broken at last by *Sous les Tentes de l'Exode* (1921),

Chansons Désabusées and *La Chanson de la Rue Saint-Paul* (1922), *Les Sept Notre-Dame des plus beaux Métiers* (1923). And this represents his finest work, for by 1922 he had become highly neurasthenic to the point of madness, and for the last years of his life he was the ailing ghost of his former self, reliving the innocent joys of his youth, shrinking from tragic memories of the death of his mother and the suicide of his sister in the 1890's, mourning his father who had been a constant source of comfort and joy until his own death in 1911, and carefully tended and protected by his man-servant and a lifelong female friend, Gabrielle, who had carefully nursed his feelings since the sudden (and for him tragic) end of a love affair in 1887.

His dash, *bonhomie* and charming manners masked a sensitive soul, and as he gave himself fully in public to enjoy the pleasures his wealth permitted him, so in private did he fully explore the lonely reaches of the mind and seek to make tolerable the intolerable by a persistent quest for that peace and tranquillity that ever eludes the grasp of material mankind. Thus it is that his poetry both troubles and captivates us, making us gladly articulate when we would otherwise have kept silent. Of his mother he writes:

> Car vous m'étiez comme Marie,
> Bien que je ne sois pas Jésus,
>
> Et lorsque vous êtes partie,
> J'ai su que j'avais tout perdu. . . .
>
> O ma mère des Ecaussines,
> C'est votre sang qui parle en moi!

For his father:

> Un jour où j'avais cru trouver
> Celle qui eût orné ma vie,
> A qui je m'étais tout donné,
> Mais qui las! ne m'a pas suivi,
>
> Alors et comme je pleurais,
> C'est vous si doux qui m'avez dit:
> Rien n'est perdu et tout renaît,
> Il est plus haut des paradis.

And then he recollects his smiling madonnas and the paintings of Van Eyck or some Flemish primitive:

> Marie, épandez vos cheveux:
> voici rire les anges bleus
>
> et dans vos bras Jésus qui bouge
> avec ses pieds et ses mains rouges,
>
> et puis encor les anges blonds
> jouant de tous leurs violons.

For him the Virgin Mary is the incarnation of purity, of motherhood, of consolation and he takes her into his confidence and chats casually and colloquially of all his worries. He is the familiar of all the rosy-cheeked angels that step from the canvases in which he delights. And he is also the familiar of the humble and meek of heart:

> Un pauvre homme est entré chez moi
> Pour des chansons qu'il venait vendre,
> Comme Pâques chantait en Flandre
> Et mille oiseaux doux à entendre,
> Un pauvre homme a chanté chez moi.

In *Les Sept Notre-Dame des plus beaux Métiers* he hymns the dignity of their daily, routine tasks; identifies himself still more closely with them and with the Antwerp of his early childhood; yearns with them for release; fixes his eyes, beyond the harbour bar and the mole with its crucifix, on the distant prospect of the sea, and with them utters his earlier prayer:

> Mon Dieu, mien, de la rue Saint-Paul,
> Donnez-moi, vous en long couché,
>
> Là-bas au calvaire du môle
> Comme aux marins que vous aimez,
>
> Le sommeil doux qu'après la vie
> J'ai de tous les temps espéré.

CHAPTER FIVE

Maurice Maeterlinck (1862-1949)

I

BETWEEN 1890 and 1911, when he was awarded the Nobel Prize for Literature, Maurice Maeterlinck was universally acclaimed as a playwright, poet and philosopher of distinction, as the most important interpreter of popular symbolism writing in the French tongue, and as the one man who had saved the French theatre from the quagmire and stagnancy into which Zola and his naturalistic school had plunged it. 'At last,' wrote the French critic, Mirbeau, 'we can leave this cellar without light or air.' In the influential pages of *Le Figaro* he made extravagant claims for *La Princesse Maleine*, implying that it was a work at least as great as anything that Shakespeare had written. It was further stated – and this at a time when Paul Verlaine, Mallarmé and Jean Moréas were still alive – that 'c'est de l'étranger, c'est de Belgique que nous viennent M. Maeterlinck, M. Verhaeren et M. Rodenbach, c'est à dire les trois noms les plus purs, les plus retentissants, les plus définitifs de la jeune poésie française'! Contemporary French authors, whilst they might speak disparagingly of this 'barbare du nord', had to concede his worth. 'Un ouvrier belge qui s'est acheté un chapeau trop petit et des culottes trop larges' is Jules Renard's verdict on Maeterlinck the man, but he has later to admit that he is 'un grand artiste à qui c'est égal d'ennuyer son lecteur . . . ton Maeterlinck, c'est sublime. On a pensé à tout ça, on n'a pas pu l'exprimer.'

Yet the award of the Nobel Prize seems to have put an end to his career and to all further expectations. From 1911 onwards both his work and reputation steadily declined, and his death in 1949 passed almost unnoticed. Very few critical studies of his work have since appeared, and the latest and fullest seems unable to whip up much enthusiasm either for Maeterlinck or for his work.[1] Is this unjust? Does he date as much as we are led to believe? Are we right in our tacit assumption that *Pelléas et Mélisande* could not have retained its appeal but for the music of Debussy? True, he borrowed much from Shakespeare. His rhymeless verses in *Serres Chaudes* were written under the inspiration of Walt Whitman's *Leaves of Grass*. He was a great admirer of the American essayist, Emerson, and wrote a preface in 1894 to a translation of seven of his master's essays. *L'Oiseau Bleu* owes much to Barrie's *Peter Pan* and is marred by similar mawkish touches. On the other hand, Yeats, Synge and Masefield came strongly in their turn under Maeterlinck's influence. So did Hugo von Hofmannsthal and Eulenberg in Germany, and Eugene O'Neill from America.

I think we have to remember that Maeterlinck began to write at a time when a firm reaction had set in against the bland materialism of the nineteenth century, and that his own peculiar nordic outlook on life, his mysticism, his uncanny art of suggestion and evocation then captured the imagination of thoughtful people. Here was no artifice, none of the classical tradition and restraint that French symbolist writers could not quite escape. As we have argued in the previous chapter, true symbolism is a poetry, not of the smiling Mediterranean shores but of the north. It was born in the Ardennes and in Catholic Flanders. And when Maeterlinck made clear his aim of creating a beauty that was truly *of the spirit* he was speaking for all the past generations of Belgian symbolists. 'Nous ne nous grandissons qu'en grandissant les mystères qui nous accablent,' he claimed. In this sense Maeterlinck was inimitable, even in his own country, and if Verhaeren has been more in fashion it is because Verhaeren soon broke away from this pure symbolistic approach and forged a new kind of romanticism that centred on modern city and industrial life. Let us not forget either that Maeterlinck early steeped himself in the writings of the fourteenth-century Dutch mystic, Van Ruysbroeck ('the soul finds God in its own depths'), whom he translated in 1891, and of the eighteenth-century German poet and philosopher, Novalis, whom he also translated in 1895.

[1] W. D. Halls: *Maurice Maeterlinck: A Study of his Life and Thoughts*, O.U.P., 1960

There was also a roundness, a completeness, a personally satisfying wholeness to Maeterlinck's philosophical outlook by the time he was awarded the Nobel Prize. He had little further exploration of his own soul to do. Whilst he sought his own spiritual repose he had been electrifying to his audiences. He had nothing more to offer them that could in the same way excite. As the modern Belgian poet Roger Bodart has pointed out, to understand Maeterlinck properly you have to think of the *corpus* of his work as a four-sided pyramid: poetry, drama, philosophy and science. Moving from one to the other we gradually pass from darkness and shade to light, from frightened intuition and panic to quiet acceptance and understanding. The first word of his work is 'fear', pronounced with a Germanic and then an English inflection. The last word is 'peace' – the mystical peace of the Fleming, the rationalistic peace of Montaigne or Fabre, the optimism of the American Christian Scientist. Such a diversified writer must at first dazzle, then bewilder, and finally satiate, particularly when he is primarily interested only in his own voyage of self-exploration. I do not think this too fanciful an interpretation. I am indeed reminded of André Gide's entry in his *Journal* for 17 March 1904. He had been dining with Verhaeren and Maeterlinck and recorded the following conversation: VERHAEREN – 'Il n'y a plus que ce que j'écris qui m'intéresse.' MAETERLINCK – 'Ce que j'écris ne m'intéresse plus beaucoup . . . Du reste, je ne travaille plus à présent que par habitude.'

We should finally do well to remember that Maeterlinck is a mystical writer and as such has nothing in common with the moralist. He is not primarily concerned with the practical results of his labours and is indifferent to their effect on others. He speaks only to those who are prepared to listen to him. 'We possess a self more profound and more boundless than the self of the passions or of pure reason,' he says. All forms of religion and all works of art are part of a great conspiracy to forget death, to transcend it, to be sure that there is something which makes it worth while to go on living. How could Maeterlinck make a present appeal to a century compelled perhaps by force of circumstance to adopt a diametrically opposed view – or at least to seem to profess it?

2

On the completion of his law studies at the University of Ghent, Maeterlinck spent several months in Paris (1886) and made the acquaintance there of Villiers de L'Isle-Adam and the leaders of the symbolist movement. He published his first poems and a curious short story, 'Le Massacre des Innocents', in the literary review *La Pléiade*. The story follows the example set by Bruegel the Elder in making Bethlehem become a sixteenth-century Flemish village. The difference from Bruegel the Elder lies in the fact that whilst Bruegel transplanted his painting to *his* century and so made it a 'modern' study, Maeterlinck situates his story three hundred years earlier than his day and uses a quaint and archaic language and style reminiscent of De Coster and *Ulenspiegel*. It was an experiment that Maeterlinck never cared to repeat.

On his return from France he busied himself, as we have already seen, in writing for *La Jeune Belgique* and *La Wallonie*. In 1889 he published his first collected verse, *Serres Chaudes*, and to this he added in 1896 *Douze Chansons*, the whole to comprise his total poetic output. His first play, *La Princesse Maleine*, appeared in 1889, and *L'Intruse* and *Les Aveugles* in 1890. *Pelléas et Mélisande* and *Intérieur* followed in 1892, and *La Mort de Tintagiles* in 1894. During this same period he issued his translations of Ruysbroeck and Novalis, prefaced the volume of essays of Emerson, and published his own first collection of essays, *Le Trésor des Humbles* (1896). It was in this latter year, at the height of his theatrical triumphs, that he settled permanently in France.

The second period of his literary activity stretches from 1896 to the outbreak of war in 1914. Here we find him gradually abandoning his idea of man as a powerless victim of the blind forces of destiny and substituting a more serene and stoical conception of existence: happiness is to be found in the discovery of the soul and by an attentive and close study of the laws of nature and of forms of life in both the animal and vegetable worlds. It is the period of the important books of essays: *La Sagesse et la Destinée* (1898); *La Vie des Abeilles* and *Le Temple Enseveli* (1901); *Le Double Jardin* (1904); *L'Intelligence des Fleurs* (1907); *La Mort*

(1913). It is also the period of a new series of plays: *Monna Vanna* (1902); *Joyzelle* (1903); *L'Oiseau Bleu* (1908); *Marie-Magdeleine* (1913).

The last period, stretching down to 1930, gives us only one play of importance, *Le Bourgmestre de Stilemonde* (1918), and further volumes of essays, the most important of which are *La Vie des Termites* (1927) and *La Vie des Fourmis* (1930). In this period he plunges himself more deeply into his metaphysical studies and becomes intensely absorbed by animal biology.

3

His poetic output, as we have noted, was strictly limited to *Serres Chaudes* and to the *Douze Chansons* he added to the former volume in 1900 on the occasion of a new edition of his collected verse.[1] *Serres Chaudes* slowly made its impact. Here was a poet who, surpassing all his contemporaries, showed that the theories propounded by the symbolists were capable of exact expression and application. He could convey complete detachment from the ordinary human world. More surely than others he could pinpoint an emotion or feeling, and, using the basic technique and device of a setting of olden times the better to bring out the kind of racial symbolism the symbolist poets believed to be inherent in all folklore, he could express the enveloping mystery of life, the ceaseless quest for the unattainable, for a free and pure and inner beauty of soul and quietism of mind and spirit:

> J'ai cherché trente ans, mes sœurs,
> Où s'est-il caché?
> J'ai marché trente ans, mes sœurs,
> Sans m'en approcher . . .
>
> J'ai marché trente ans, mes sœurs,
> Et mes pieds sont las,
> Il était partout, mes sœurs,
> Et n'existe pas . . .

---

[1] *Douze Chansons* first appeared in 1896. There were *fifteen* poems in all.

> L'heure est triste enfin, mes sœurs,
> Otez vos sandales,
> Le soir meurt aussi, mes sœurs,
> Et mon âme a mal . . .
>
> Vous avez seize ans, mes sœurs,
> Allez loin d'ici,
> Prenez mon bourdon, mes sœurs,
> Et cherchez aussi . . .

All his verse indicates the kind of moral climate that is to be the setting for his later work. He is oppressed by a great sadness. He is preoccupied with the mysteries of earthly existence and its seeming futility:

> Examinez au clair de lune!
> (Oh, rien n'y est à sa place!)
> On dirait une folle devant les juges,
> Un navire de guerre à pleines voiles sur un canal,
> Des oiseaux de nuit sur des lys,
> Un glas vers midi,
> (Là-bas sous ces cloches!)
> Une étape de malades dans la prairie,
> Une odeur d'éther un jour de soleil.
>
> Mon Dieu! mon Dieu! quand aurons-nous la pluie,
> Et la neige et le vent dans la serre?

He examines with loving care all the beauty with which he is surrounded only to find that it means nothing:

> Les fleurs s'effeuillent une à une
> Sur le reflet du firmament,
> Pour descendre éternellement
> Dans l'eau du songe et dans la lune.

He expects a mystical transformation in the soul of man, an awakening from sleep, and this, he feels, can only be brought about by some power outside man's own soul – '*your* fingers on *my* face':

Mon âme en est triste à la fin;
Elle est triste enfin d'être lasse,
Elle est lasse enfin d'être en vain,
Elle est triste et lasse à la fin
Et j'attends vos mains sur ma face.

J'attends vos doigts purs sur ma face,
Pareils à des anges de glace,
J'attends qu'ils m'apportent l'anneau;
J'attends leur fraîcheur sur ma face,
Comme un trésor au fond de l'eau.

Et j'attends enfin leurs remèdes
Pour ne pas mourir au soleil,
Mourir sans espoir au soleil!
J'attends qu'ils lavent mes yeux tièdes
Où tant de pauvres ont sommeil!

Serres Chaudes contained little more than thirty poems, and these were interspersed with seven longer pieces without rhyme or metre and written most obviously under the inspiration of *Leaves of Grass*. Most of the poems are written in octosyllabic quatrains, but a number of these betray again the influence of Whitman, who once referred to his method of presentation as 'a perpetual series of what might be called ejaculations'. Maeterlinck could have made the same claim: his rhymeless verses are the freest of *vers libres* of their time and easily abreast of Whitman's own emanicipated lines:

Et ces regards insolites!
Il y en a sous la voûte desquels on assiste à l'exécution d'une vierge
    dans une salle close,
Et ceux qui font songer à des tristesses ignorées!
A des paysans aux fenêtres de l'usine,
A un jardinier devenu tisserand,
A une après-midi d'été dans un musée de cires,
Aux idées d'une reine qui regarde un malade dans le jardin,
A une odeur de camphre dans la forêt,
A enfermer une princesse dans une tour, un jour de fête,
A naviguer toute une semaine sur un canal tiède.

Here is the 'catalogue style' of Whitman to perfection. But Maeterlinck is much more subtly and delicately involved than was usually the case with Whitman. Symbolism has been described by Tancred de Visan as using a succession of accumulated images in order to exteriorize lyrical intuition. In this respect Maeterlinck is the last and most evocative of the Symbolists. Note the 'princesse dans une tour' and the force of this in its context. Note also a return to the image of sailing on a placid canal. *Serres Chaudes* is the poet's revolt against the stifling and placid provincialism of his native Ghent. Emancipation left him with nothing further to say on this score. And *Serres Chaudes* itself carried symbolism to its furthest point of perfection and subtly introduced the newer surrealist techniques. Maeterlinck's importance, at least as far as Belgian poets are concerned, is that he freed them from traditional forms and in so doing forced them to be themselves. Modern Belgian poetry begins with Maeterlinck.

4

It must be unique in the history of the theatre for a man suddenly to burst from obscurity to recognition and fame on the strength of one play, *La Princesse Maleine*, which, as far as I am aware, has never yet been publicly performed. Maeterlinck first published his play in serial form in 1889 and in two private and limited editions in 1890. He sent a copy of the play to Mallarmé, who passed it to the critic Octave Mirbeau, and he, on the front page of *Le Figaro* for 24 August 1890, trumpeted it to fame. Maeterlinck had dared to write a play which was not

> un chef-d'œuvre étiqueté chef-d'œuvre à l'avance, comme en publient tous les jours nos jeunes maîtres, chantés sur tous les tons de la glapissante lyre – ou plutôt de la glapissante flûte contemporaine; mais un admirable et pur et éternel chef-d'œuvre, un chef-d'œuvre qui suffit à immortaliser un nom et à faire bénir ce nom par tous les affamés du beau et du grand; un chef-d'œuvre comme les artistes honnêtes et tourmentés, parfois, aux heures d'enthousiasme ont rêvé d'en écrire un, et comme ils n'en ont écrit aucun jusqu'ici.

What Maeterlinck had in effect dared to do was to take an exactly opposite course to everything fashionable in the theatre at that moment. To the naturalistic school of writing – the school that believed profoundly in providing 'tranches de vie' and exact imitations of nature – he opposed a disregard and disdain for exactitude, for truth, and even for likelihood. The setting for *La Princesse Maleine* is a purely imaginary Holland with no location in time, and the young heroine is herself surrounded by incest and the most atrocious of crimes. Wind, thunderstorms, flashing comets and falling stars, mysterious knockings and omens of all kinds together build up a sense of the occult and the supernatural and create through a kind of infectious delirium both a sense of fear and of the truly tragic. It is all a glorious hotch-potch, of course, borrowed freely and adapted from *Lear*, from *Hamlet* and from *Macbeth*. The wicked Queen Anne (Lady Macbeth) is opposed to the sweet and innocent Maleine (Ophelia). Yet it is much more than mere plagiarism. It is a theatre of suggestion rather than direct statement, and the language of the play has a wonderful, dream-like and haunting beauty. What he intends is an allegory of life hinted at through ambiguous dialogue and symbolical stage effects and visually presented in poetic settings such as vaguely medieval castles and impenetrable forests. It is, in fact, the atmosphere of the early Yeats, who owes a good deal to Maeterlinck's influence.

This desire to present an allegory of life led to a still further innovation, that of conducting his plays on two levels, one of reality where the action can be seen and one where it is only expressed through signs. This technique in turn allowed him to put forward his belief in the transcendental self; his conviction that intelligence alone does not bring us to identify ourselves with the good, but only our subconscious, our presentiments, our fears, sympathies and instinctive repulsions. Man lives on two planes, he would maintain: the one of conscious, material activity; the other of involuntary action, and this is the more important – it is fundamental and eternal. Thus all his characters have pregnant silences, and even in speaking they imply much more than they state explicitly. It is the theatre of the *sous-entendus*, the theatre that inspired Eugene O'Neill to write *Strange Interlude*, for example, and as such it puts forward a conception of art vitally opposed to all that realism stood for.

Again, a play by Maeterlinck is at one and the same time a dialogue of ideas and a series of symbols. His characters are made to develop his own conception of the world – a sombre and fatalistic conception haunted by the problems of death and destiny. In the earlier plays his characters cannot escape from the exterior force which controls their lives. They may understand exactly where they are being driven but they cannot change their course. He believed that men and women were mere marionettes who jerked and mouthed for a little under the direction of mysterious and supernatural forces, and he claimed, in consequence, that these early plays of his were intended for marionette performances.

It was the combination of all these new and often startling effects that subtly built up a sense of suspense, of fear, of tragedy quite alien to the theatre of Maeterlinck's day. It also provided moments of intense dramatic effectiveness that in this particular sense could be said to have had no parallel since Shakespeare. One is reminded in this respect of one extraordinary scene in *La Princesse Maleine*: the murderers are on stage, next to the little princess who has just been killed; a knock is heard on the door; it is the nurse who, through the closed door, speaks tenderly to Maleine; the murderers are frozen to rigidity, stricken with terror at the thought of possible discovery. It was a device Maeterlinck was to use again and again in different plays with the same telling dramatic effect.

Note also how his peculiar use of symbolism in the theatre, allied to his lack of a positive religious faith and his belief in the unseen forces of destiny, has its own tense and highly dramatic contribution to make. When Maleine is murdered all the swans fly away except one which mysteriously falls down dead. In the play, *L'Intruse*, the family of a dangerously sick woman are waiting in the next room the arrival of a relative. The nightingales stop singing. The sound of a scythe being sharpened is heard. There is the noise of a door suddenly opening. Later it is revealed that whilst they were talking Death has come and taken the woman away. The important point is that none of these symbolistic effects *need* be interpreted in any supernatural way.

Each is *capable* of a rational explanation. There is no *deus ex machina* contrivance. Therein lies the terror.

L'Intruse, a one-act play, and the first of Maeterlinck's plays to be performed, was the last item in a benefit matinée performance for Paul Verlaine and the painter Paul Gauguin given on 21 May 1891. The distinguished producer, Lugné-Poë, was responsible for its inclusion in the bill. The performance caused an immediate sensation and led to a long and fruitful collaboration between Maeterlinck and Lugné-Poë. December of the same year saw the creation of *Les Aveugles* with Lugné-Poë himself acting the principal part of the oldest of the blind men. The plot is simple and Death is again the protagonist. An old priest who is taking a group of blind men and women for a walk suddenly collapses and dies. Helpless and abandoned, the blind are a prey to many terrors, not least the terror in their own minds. A climax is reached when a stranger finally approaches who turns out to be none other than Death himself. Intuitional knowledge of the fate awaiting the group is possessed both by the oldest of the blind men, who is a kind of seer, and by the only sighted person in the group, a helpless young baby who cries aloud as the mysterious stranger approaches. Though possessed of this knowledge, neither the baby nor the blind man can do a thing to remedy the situation. You are left to interpret the play as you will. Presumably the priest represents the Church and the blind the plight of forsaken humanity. . . . How much does Beckett's *Waiting for Godot* owe, however indirectly, to Maeterlinck? It is certainly a variation on the same theme.

Lugné-Poë's production of *Pelléas et Mélisande* in 1893 spared no effort to capture the out-of-time and out-of-place atmosphere inherent in the play as Maeterlinck had conceived it. It was a tremendous success in Paris, in Rotterdam and in The Hague. It was ridiculed in Brussels. None the less, this first important and major success encouraged Maeterlinck to grant permission to Debussy to compose a score for the play and gave him a certain assurance and confidence in his own ability that had so far been lacking. After the production of *Pelléas et Mélisande*, Maeterlinck gradually abandons his fundamental attitude of despair and turns in more optimistic mood to try to understand the nature and purpose of existence. In other words, he now allows himself to be guided by his own genius and not by pessimistic superstition.

The story of *Pelléas et Mélisande* is once again simple. The elder grandson of King Arkel, lost in a mighty forest, finds the beautiful and innocent Mélisande weeping by a spring. He brings her as his bride to his grandfather's castle, close by the sea. There, the younger brother, Pelléas, in turn falls in love with Mélisande and she returns his love. The jealous elder brother surprises them one moonlit evening in what they had intended to be a farewell embrace. He kills Pelléas but only wounds Mélisande. None the less she dies, not of the wound but because 'elle était née . . . sans raison . . . pour mourir, et elle meurt sans raison'. A banal, sensational newspaper story, but a story that the symbolistic devices of Maeterlinck work upon to produce a heroic and tragic theme. Mélisande, pure and innocent, brings love pure and unalloyed into the bleak fastness of King Arkel's castle. For a little while warmth and gladness permeate this drab little world. Love challenges Death and is worsted. The puppets on their strings play out the grim yet beautiful charade.

Intérieur and *La Mort de Tintagiles* betray an identical conception of drama and have the same tight unity about them. There is the same Love–Death theme, the same timelessness, the same challenge. They are, however, the last of the puppet plays. And *Intérieur* is noteworthy in that it is purely 'static' theatre. Nothing happens. A group of people are carrying the body of a drowned girl to her home where her unsuspecting family are making merry.

The plays of Maeterlinck's second and non-pessimistic period betray a marked change of course. He abandons the Flemish traditional setting for a more orthodox Latin approach. He is searching for clarity, for a kind of happy harmony, and his characters, as a result, cease to float around in a kind of no-man's-land between this world and some other, and find solid ground. He frees himself from the symbolistic 'fog' and the small and cluttering mysteries. He tends to use Ibsen as his model and to capture something of the latter's clear, rapid dialogue, simple action, and intense moral sense. As far as Maeterlinck is concerned, drama must henceforth treat mainly of moral or philosophical problems. His characters are no longer puppets and begin to have a deep, psychological interest.

Of these plays, *Monna Vanna*, first produced in 1902, is easily
the most outstanding and probably the best play he ever wrote.
It depicts the difficulties and perplexities of three principal
characters in face of a series of impossible situations. It is a
historical melodrama, but one in which Maeterlinck succeeded
in exercising admirable restraint, and one which he manages to
invest with great dignity and very real pathos. The characters
are drawn firmly and convincingly and with a masterly economy
of words. The scene is Renaissance Italy in all its colourfulness
and new vigour of life. Pisa is besieged by a Florentine army, and
to save the city Monna Vanna consents to spend one night with
the mercenary leader of the besieging army, a certain Prinzivalle.
Her husband, Guido, is outraged at her decision and tells her
roughly to be gone. When she reaches the Florentine lines
Prinzivalle recognizes her as one he has dearly loved since
childhood. Naturally, he does not ravish her, and to save him she
takes him back with her to Pisa. Guido will not believe she has
not been ravished, and this 'infidelity' on the part of her husband
kills her love for him which is now transferred to the honourable
Prinzivalle. To save Prinzivalle she has to pretend that he has
indeed ravished her, that she hates him for it, and to claim that
she alone has the right to wreak her own vengeance. Prinzivalle
is cast into a dungeon of which she only has the keys. Thus she
plans to escape with Prinzivalle to happiness, and the curtain
falls as she explains to him that all that has passed is but an evil
dream; the beautiful dream is about to begin! A most effective
curtain.

A dramatist of less genius than Maeterlinck would have
treated Guido with less sympathy, the better to emphasize the
contrast between his lack of public spirit and Monna Vanna's
heroism. Maeterlinck, however, chooses to portray the poignant
tragedy of a man whose domestic life is ruined by circumstances
before which he is powerless. We see clearly that it is Guido who
must suffer most. Monna Vanna, on the other hand, is carried
away by the very inspiration of her own heroism. And this very
act straightway introduces a new and important change of theme
in this new cycle of plays: Love, though it may not absolutely
triumph over Destiny, can elude it. *Joyzelle*, first produced in
1903, introduces us to another *femme forte* who once again

proclaims Love to be the supreme justification and so evades all the snares by which Destiny would seek to destroy her.

And now, as though determined to show that in his new mood he had not lost his cunning with former symbolistic effects, Maeterlinck slowly pieced together from an earlier fairy story he had written for children his *L'Oiseau Bleu*. It was first produced in 1907 – at the Arts Theatre in Moscow – came to Paris in 1908, and then went on to win world-wide approval and to amuse audiences of children of all ages down to the late 1920's. It is an exquisite piece of work in which Maeterlinck succeeds admirably in adapting his poetry to the level of a child's imagination, pushes over an important moral lesson (true happiness is to be found at home), and cunningly combines realism with both humour and fantasy. The story of the play is too well known to need retelling. The quest of two young children for happiness brings them back home, but in the course of their quest they have learned that simple pleasures are the best; that Man is gradually conquering disease and will eventually subdue the hostile forces of Nature; that the dead are not really dead, for they live on in our memories.

A further play, this time with a Biblical theme, occupied him from 1908 onwards, and *Marie-Magdeleine* was finally produced first at Leipzig (1910) and much later in France in 1913. Again we have the *femme forte* in the courtesan who, loved by a young soldier who has the power to save Christ if she will give herself to him, refuses. It is Divine Love that is now in question. If she surrenders to the Roman officer she indulges her sexual love and by so doing saves the *body* of Christ but destroys His work; if she refuses she destroys the body of Christ, resists her own sensuous appetites and helps establish the Kingdom of Christ on earth. The last act of the play, based on her renunciation that condemns Christ to the judgement of Pilate, is tense with profound psychological portrayal of the state of mind of the various protagonists.

Maeterlinck's last play of any real importance, *Le Bourgmestre de Stilemonde*, was conceived and written during a period of mounting patriotic fervour and indignation against 'Hun' atrocities during World War I. First produced in Buenos Aires in 1918, it became known as *the* great war play. After the war it was banned in France because of the violence of the sentiments expressed, and it was later the principal cause of Maeterlinck's departure from neutral Portugal to exile in the United States between 1940 and 1947: Maeterlinck genuinely feared capture and summary execution (because of the play) at the hands of the Germans. For this last great play he returns to a setting in his native Flanders. A Flemish village is occupied by an Uhlan regiment, and one of the officers is the son-in-law of the burgomaster. An old and innocent villager is accused of shooting a brutal Prussian officer. The burgomaster refuses to sanction the execution of the villager and is executed in his place on the orders of the German Commander. Once again we have all the simple ingredients of a typical Maeterlinck tragedy: the problem of self-sacrifice; the value of one human life as weighed against another; death as dependent on chance or destiny; the triumph of love (in this case disguised as patriotism) over a brooding and apparently inescapable destiny.

True symbolism in the theatre was born and died with Maeterlinck. That much is certainly true, and it is on this premiss that Maeterlinck's influence as a playwright has usually been reduced to that of preparing the way for the later symbolic and deeply religious dramas of Paul Claudel. This judgement, particularly when viewed in the light of modern developments in the theatre and elsewhere, seems to me incomplete. With his 'static' plays, for example, Maeterlinck prepared the way for modern experimental approaches. His symbolic theatre, leading into his later period, was a forerunner of what I am tempted to call the 'theatre of anti-symbolism', of which the Belgian playwright, Henri Soumagne, provides some outstanding examples. We shall discuss this aspect later, however, in its proper place and in some detail. Again, it is surely not too fanciful to remind ourselves that Maeterlinck, in claiming that the stage is the place where masterpieces die and that the actor's personality must not obtrude – that ideally the actor ought to be suppressed entirely – was anticipating the present vogue for the anti-novel, the 'apoème', and the Beckett type of play ridiculed so mercilessly in Anouilh's *Huluberlu*.

Finally, and most important, Maeterlinck postulated the relativity of moral behaviour and on a basis of this relativity built up the whole of his dramatic tensions: what is genuinely true for one character becomes automatically false in the eyes of another. Each individual is isolated in his own world and nobody speaks the same language. Thus, in *Pelléas et Mélisande*, just before dying Mélisande utters the words: 'Non, non, nous n'avons pas été coupables.' From the point of view of Pelléas and Mélisande it is nothing but the truth; from the point of view of the elder brother, however, it is a shameless travesty of the truth. Modern playwrights exploit the dramatic possibilities of this situation again and again.

5

The prose writings of Maeterlinck are a direct, sincere and often moving expression of a man afraid of the void and unable to accept the uniqueness of the Christian religion. His is a perpetual quest for the kindness and sweetness that the religion he rejects tells him is God's especial grace accorded to man. He looks for this kindness and sweetness among the humble; he studies life in the animal and insect world and among the flowers to see what message or hope of release they can give; he is in perpetual quest for his own soul and for the meaning of existence; and he consoles himself the while by a fatalistic acceptance of his destiny. He fails, of course, to penetrate the mysteries of Destiny and Death. Nor does he discover the universal secret of Wisdom and Truth. No matter. In the process of searching he distils for us pages of poetic beauty and poignant emotion alongside others of gentle irony and calm acceptance and serenity of mind.

His first published collection of essays, *Le Trésor des Humbles*, is mainly concerned with the mystical discovery of the soul and represents in the author an upsurge of optimism and of faith in the future. He maintains that the sins of the body cannot injure the soul since it is inviolable, and he expresses the hope that this exploratory voyage in search of the soul will one day make everything known; though we are presently groping in the dark we must not relax our endeavours. The soul, indeed, can only be awakened by the efforts of the individual. However, a special effort is required, for souls communicate in silence, and only very

occasionally do their deepest and truest thoughts rise to consciousness and utterance. This central idea of the virtues of
silence, taken originally from Carlyle, leads on to some of his
most profound, disturbing and captivating utterances:

> Il ne faut pas croire que la parole serve jamais aux communi-
> cations véritables entre les êtres. . . . Dès que nous avons vraiment
> *quelque chose à nous dire*, nous sommes *obligés* de nous taire. . . .
> Nous ne parlons qu'aux heures où nous ne vivons pas, dans les
> moments où *nous ne voulons pas* apercevoir nos frères et où nous
> nous sentons à une grande distance de la réalité. Et dès que nous
> parlons, quelque chose nous prévient que des portes divines se
> ferment quelque part. . . . Les paroles passent entre les hommes,
> mais le silence, s'il a eu un moment l'occasion d'être actif, ne
> s'efface jamais, et la vie véritable, et la seule qui laisse quelque
> trace, n'est faite que de silence. . . . S'il vous est donné de
> descendre un instant en votre âme, jusqu'aux profondeurs
> habitées par les anges, ce qu'avant tout vous vous rappellerez
> d'un être aimé profondément, ce n'est pas les paroles qu'il a dites
> ou les gestes qu'il a faits, mais les silences que vous avez vécus
> ensemble; car c'est la *qualité* de ces silences qui seule a révélé la
> *qualité* de votre amour et de vos âmes.

La Sagesse et la Destinée, published two years later, earned him
extravagant praise in Germany, where he was compared with
Nietzsche, and also came to be widely translated and read
throughout Europe generally. His style is firmer and more lucid
and yet retains all the poetic charm and quality associated with
the earlier work. It is a step further forward in the process of self-
knowing and shows Maeterlinck at grips with his pessimistic
fears and overcoming them. He affirms that man, by developing
the good that is within him, may bring happiness to himself.
Destiny, therefore, ceases to be a nightmare-spectre, and
Maeterlinck advances gradually towards the triumphant statement made in *La Mort* (1913) that the Infinite cannot will evil
for us. In effect, the essays are a kind of meditation on the
connexion between Wisdom and Destiny. Wisdom, he affirms, is
above and beyond Reason – is a kind of mystical power that can
conquer Destiny or, at the very least, protect the soul against its
blows. As in the earlier work, the approach is near-pagan, and

the Wisdom he speaks of is closely tied up with a mystical conception of a God who is in everyone and to be found everywhere for the seeking, manifest both in space and in time. His attitude is very much of a Stoic (*à la* Montaigne) trying to live with the idea of death and dreaming his dreams of heroism. Undoubtedly it was this aspect of the work as a whole which particularly endeared him to his German readers already responding to the Nietzschean claim that 'every conquest, every step forward in knowledge, is the outcome of courage, of hardness, of cleanliness towards oneself'.

Maeterlinck may, as he claimed, have been uninfluenced by Nietzsche, but his next two books, *La Vie des Abeilles* and *L'Intelligence des Fleurs*, show him rejecting Nietzsche's 'bungled and botched' human beings and looking in the insect and plant world for a manifestation of the supreme intelligence that leads to happiness and perfection. By remarking all that is significant and beautiful in the lives and habits of bees and plants Maeterlinck attempts to bring us to a wider perception of life. His philosophy, as expressed in these two books, is very calm and very idealistic. He arrives at the conclusion that there is a close affinity between man and nature. Both betray a high degree of intelligence, but if that intelligence is of a better quality in man it may be that man is merely a better conductor for the supreme intelligence (the Creator) that governs all things and holds the key to the mystery of Life. The struggle, therefore, is to attain full communion with this supreme intelligence, and Maeterlinck teaches forgetfulness of self in this struggle, urging that if man faithfully does his duty with regard to both himself and his fellows, he ennobles that duty. The bees do not know whether they will eat the honey they have harvested. In the same way we do not know who will profit by the spiritual influence we introduce into the universe. As there is something infinitely beautiful in the constant, provident activity of the bees, so there is something sublime in man's unremitting cultivation of the good within him.

La Vie des Abeilles is neither a treatise on apiculture nor a collection of scientific observations and discoveries. As he himself puts it,

D

Qui aura lu ce livre ne sera pas en état de conduire une ruche, mais connaîtra à peu près tout ce qu'on sait de certain, de curieux, de profound et d'intime sur ses habitants.

The book might in a certain light be considered as a thinly veiled social satire, but it goes much further than that. For Maeterlinck the swarming of the bees is a moving testimony of the love of the present generation for the future one for which it gladly sacrifices itself. And the swarming of the bees leads Maeterlinck to the conclusion that nature, in its effort to perpetuate itself, affords proof of a prodigious intelligence. Similarly, the idea behind *L'Intelligence des Fleurs* is that, like us, plants must fight against the obscure forces of Destiny which tries to crush them, and that, like us, they strive constantly for a freer and more glorious existence.

La Vie des Termites* and *La Vie des Fourmis* are both cast in more sombre tones and notably lack the flights of poetic beauty of the earlier volumes. In a sense, the very choice of these insects for a close study is symbolic. Maeterlinck, towards the end of his life, has come to realize that his earlier optimism of: 'Cherchez, mes frères, cherchez et vous trouverez!' was misplaced. The ultimate goal is unattainable and the purpose of existence must remain shrouded in mystery. But it is not the solution that is important. It is the search, even knowing there can be no solution. And this search is 'le plus noble effort que l'homme soit à même de tenter avant sa mort'. Maeterlinck might reject all practised forms of religion but he is still convinced of the existence of God. Like Pascal, however, he is overawed by the final mystery of God:

Plus j'avance, plus il recule ses limites. Plus je réfléchis, moins je le comprends. Plus je le regarde, moins je le vois, et moins je le vois, plus je suis sûr qu'il existe; car s'il n'existe pas, c'est le néant partout, et qui peut concevoir que le néant existe?

Man, like the termites and the ants, has erected a moral, political and social code of behaviour – one which even involves extinction, just as the termites make war on the ants – yet one which keeps him busily tunnelling the darkness about him and moving, however obscurely, towards the light.

6

Whatever may be the final verdict on Maeterlinck, his importance to his age and generation cannot lightly be dismissed. A harsh critic might deny that his works can seriously be considered as philosophy, but he must admit that they have a genuine and very great beauty. He may be irritated by the inconclusiveness of his teaching and feel that he never lost the vagueness which was a characteristic of his earlier plays. He may accuse him of merely embroidering word-tapestries for our delight. He should remember, however, that Maeterlinck's attitude to life was that of a mystic and not of an analyst; that he is concerned throughout with the ideal and with the mysteries of life as they appear to the poet; that his theories, in consequence, are poetic rather than scientific. Maeterlinck was important in that he taught us nothing which we did not know, but stressed rather what we had known, should have known, and had forgotten. Perhaps he will come into his own again. Perhaps his message will again be heard in our own troubled times as we search for our own particular Blue Bird. And perhaps then, with Tyltyl, we may again exclaim:

L'oiseau, mais il est bleu! Mais c'est ma tourterelle! . . . Mais elle est bien plus bleue que quand je suis parti! Mais c'est là l'Oiseau Bleu que nous avons cherché. . . .

CHAPTER SIX

The Modern Flemish Novel

I

THE MODERN Flemish novel may be said to follow one of two paths: either it cheapens itself in a somewhat frenzied effort to follow the injunction of Conscience to teach the people to read and be proud of their heritage, or it follows the academic line first laid down by Vermeylen and successfully developed by Herman Teirlinck. For the first part of the twentieth century, however, Buysse and Streuvels were most in vogue and the realist novel of peasant life tended to dominate and invite the not unjust criticism from abroad that Flemish literature had become exclusively regional and even parochial. The two most popular authors following in this tradition were Félix Timmermans and Ernest Claes, and because of their strong narrative sense, their racy and pictorial style and their desire to amuse rather than instruct, they tended to have a wide reading public even outside Flanders and so create the impression that the Flemish novel, as an art form, could progress no further. As a result, the more stylistic writings of Willem Elsschot and the greater artifice he commanded in exploring the more subtle aspects of life, on a non-regionalist basis, were ignored.

A swing-over to the more intellectual and universal approach to the novel that Vermeylen had advocated only came in the period between the two wars with the publication of the deeply psychological novels of Maurice Roelants. Even then, however, the 'popular' novel persisted, and if its chief exponents – Gerard Walschap, Filip de Pillecijn and Marnix Gijsen – are stylists and take great care to give artistic unity to all they write, they nevertheless tend to be too romantically preoccupied with social problems and thus to cheapen their craft. We have, in point of fact, had to wait for a present generation of promising young writers, typified by Johan Daisne and Louis-Paul Boom, to feel that the promise of *Van Nu En Straks* and the line of development sketched in by Teirlinck is coming to real fruition in terms of the contemporary scene.

2

Félix TIMMERMANS (1886–1947) has the doubtful reputation of having written compelling novels, centred mainly on his native Lierre and peopled with half-real, half-imagined characters living life in all its coarseness with gusto and enjoyment, which have been eagerly read outside Belgium and taken to be truly representative of the Fleming temperament and Flemish way of life. Yet Timmermans is neither a realist nor in any sense an accurate chronicler of events. He is incurably romantic, roguish and idealistic in his approach, and it is his uncanny narrative skill that makes everything he says carry conviction. His imagination is often unbridled, and he presents his characters in a witty and affectionate manner.

His greatest work is undoubtedly *Pallieter* which he had the good fortune to publish in 1917 when Europe, saddened by the privations of an apparently interminable war, had lost all interest in the beauties of life and nature and all real zest for living. Timmermans' hero, Pallieter, is a swashbuckling egoist, devoid of any intellectual pretensions, a fine brute of a man, who enjoys life to the full and does everything on a large scale. He eats and drinks more than anyone else; he sings well; he plays all kinds of musical instruments. He is a truculent Rabelaisian character – a fleshy creation almost straight from a Jordaens painting.

The next year, Timmermans showed his versatility of approach by abandoning the violence of Jordaens to give a discreet Bruegel's detail of Flemish village life in *Het Kindeken Jezus in Vlaanderen* ('The Child Jesus in Flanders'). The theme is simple, direct and yet mystical: it is the moving story of the childhood of Jesus as though He had been reared amongst a simple-minded and idealized Flemish peasantry.

Finally, we should note his *Anne-Marie* (1922) which depicts still another facet of his imaginative skill. Here he paints life in a small, old-world provincial setting of drinking, poetizing, womanizing, yet amidst which can suddenly burst and flower the tender love of two very charming people. Here Timmermans is matchless for his skill in harmonizing grossness and fullness of exuberant living with sentimentality that is made captivatingly acceptable.

Ernest CLAES (1885–) is the author of a crowd of novels and short stories either inspired by war recollections, or drawn from folklore and the lives of the villagers inhabiting his native Campine. Amongst his short stories the *Vulgaire Geshiedenis van Charelke Dop* ('The Commonplace Story of Charelke Dop') and *Clémentine* are probably the best known. The former is a satirical description of a war profiteer, and the latter describes the state of mind of a servant who dreams of becoming the sole heiress of her employers. The novel that made him famous was *De Witte* ('The Flaxen-haired Boy'). It was published in 1920 and a film was made of it in 1934. The young boy, Filasse, is a kind of Mark Twain character, a Tom Sawyer, a roguish fellow whose adventures are told with verve, humour and not a little cynicism.

Willem ELSSCHOT (1882–) is a native of Antwerp, and if he has become known as the chronicler of the Antwerp middle class he is, however, not a regionalist in the sense that Claes or Timmermans can be claimed as regionalists. Indeed, it is hard to fit him into any school. He writes in good and pure Dutch with almost classical simplicity and restraint. His style is direct, simple and unadorned. It has great power and charm. He needs few characters for his stories and he most obviously draws them from amongst his own friends and relatives – from his own little world that he knows so intimately and whose weaknesses and foibles he has so searchingly and ironically explored. In this sense he is usually claimed as being a biographical novelist. He sees the family as being the foundation on which spiritual, ethical and material values so much depend, and yet he sees it, ironically, as an institution whose ideal can never be other than that of the careful amassing of wealth. With this general theme and this limited motive for existence he yet manages to depict a variety of unsuspected human reactions and to transform the most ordinary individual into a figure of dramatic importance.[1]

[1] In England, C. P. Snow works not dissimilarly.

His first novel, *Villa des Roses*, was published in 1913 and is largely autobiographical in that it depicts the daily happenings in a French boarding house where he lived for a time as a young accountant. All the manias and passions of the various inhabitants are mordantly described in a gallery of unforgettable portraits. In his next major work, *Lijmen* ('Limed' – i.e. 'caught', 'taken in'), published in 1924, he turns to the world of big business and its publicity campaigns. The hero, Karel Boorman, is almost a Balzacian creation, a genial and unscrupulous swindler who exploits the credulity of his clients to the full, and who appears again in another story, this time of fiscal fraud, *Het Tankschip* ('The Tanker'), published in 1942. Elsschot's latest and most mature story – a short story – highlights perhaps best of all his peculiar genius. It is called *Het Dwaallicht* ('Will-o'-the-Wisp') and it was published in 1946. In a very few words Elsschot contrives an unforgettable picture of a rainy night in Antwerp. The 'I' of the story leaves home to buy a newspaper. Three Indian seamen approach him and show him the address of a girl working on their ship who has invited them to her home. The 'I' character helps them in their search – which proves fruitless. That is all, but this expedition in the dreary night with its melancholy close-ups and tragi-comic sequences is one long drama of loneliness.

To sum up, Elsschot's peculiar talent lies in his ability to depict the drama of the *petite bourgeoisie*: the bitter disappointments of the ordinary man with his vanities, his prejudices, his unscrupulousness, his false feelings of shame. His genius lies in the way he does this without any striving for effect, but simply, sincerely, directly. He has the courage to invite the reader's co-operation to complete with him what he starts and the skill and knowledge of human nature to compel co-operation. He is unique in Flemish literature and deserves a much wider public.

3

Marnix Gijsen (1899–　) began his career as a poet and critic but afterwards turned to the writing of what are really all autobiographical novels. He discusses in detail the hypocritical surroundings of his youth, adolescence, the death of a beloved person, the spiritual damage caused by army life. His masterpiece so far has been *Joachim van Babylon* (1948) in which he depicts the mental and physical tensions consequent upon a disastrous marriage failure. In *De Man van Overmorgen* ('The Man of the Day after Tomorrow', 1949) he is concerned (as was Maeterlinck) with the relative nature of good and evil. He is a severe but not a condescending moralist, and he has a common-sense approach to all the problems he raises. His direct, clear and restrained style is reminiscent of Elsschot, but he is too 'self-involved' in what he writes to achieve the same maturity and stature as a novelist.

Filip de PILLECIJN (1891–   ) is a genuine romantic who has tended to specialize in historical themes, but who is also much interested in psychological motivation and who carefully cultivates a polished prose style. His prose is sensitive, poetic and often symbolic. He anxiously avoids violent expressions or spasmodic phrasing. None the less, he is a popular novelist in the vein of Conscience, though he is also anxious to instruct and show how natural surroundings and historical events shape the lives and emotional reactions of those subjected to these forces. *Blauwbaard* ('Bluebeard', 1931) and *De Soldaat Johan* ('Soldier John', 1939) are novels about the Middle Ages, and it is this latter novel that thrusts him particularly into the Conscience tradition. Two other noteworthy books, *Hans van Malmédy* (1935) and the short but very subtle *Monsieur Harwarden* (1935) deal with the eighteenth century and the Napoleonic period.

Gerard WALSCHAP (1898–   ), however, dominates this generation of authors and his influence has been as considerable as his output. He is almost by instinct the 'born' novelist. All he writes is full of life and movement. He is far less concerned with nature than with man and he draws an interesting picture of human behaviour, basing most of his characters on acquaintances of his childhood when he lived in his father's grocery store and *estaminet* in his native Brabant village of Londerzeel. He immediately captures his reader's attention and holds him spellbound to the end of the story. His manner is that of the chronicler, passing without transition from direct to indirect speech – graphic, dramatic, concise. There are no long digressions, no wearisome descriptions, no deep psychological involvement as with Roelants, whom we shall discuss in a moment. All is sacrificed to pace and action. Furthermore, as is common with such novelists, he studies the extremes of human behaviour, particularly in his earlier works such as *Waldo* (1928) and the trilogy *De Familie Roothooft* (1939). He is, however, deeply interested in all important problems of man and society as the titles of some of his more important works suggest: *Trouwen* ('Marriage', 1933); *Celibaat* ('Celibacy', 1934); *Bejegening van Christus* ('Meeting Christ', 1940).

His masterpiece is *Houtekiet* (1939), in which he describes life in a kind of utopian village community on the margin limits of our own civilization. The hero is motivated by instinct alone, a fine primitive type with neither moral or religious scruples, who lives out his life in perfect harmony with nature. Here Walschap is sketching in his concept of an ideal community – a Rousseau-like picture – and he forces his reader, as always, to take sides. With Walschap it is impossible to remain impartial. And as throughout his novels and short stories he treats in dramatic fashion of the existence of God, of the relationship of Church with State, of the problems of Christian as opposed to State education, of the problems of the organization of society with all its prejudices and customs, so must the reader accept or reject the solution propounded to the issues involved and accept or reject Walschap.

The most subtle and the most gifted of this generation of writers, however, is Maurice ROELANTS (1895–). Instead of following the beaten path and describing man and his dominant passions from the outside he is the first to introduce his Flemish reader to the psychological novel – a novel in which, whilst there is little or no action, all the inner compulsions motivating a person's behaviour and eventually leading to some kind of action are microscopically examined with consummate skill, finesse and discretion. Roelants sets himself the task of exploring all that is *behind* the little everyday dramas of modern existence for the ordinary individual. He is in the same tradition as Madame de La Fayette or François Mauriac. And he has the same careful regard for style. Nothing useless, forced or artificial is allowed to intrude. He has his characters all the time under perfect control and he does not allow the action to dominate and intrude a strident note into the subtle harmonies he has devised.

Similarly, his themes all revolve around the eternal triangle situation. He never needs more than three or four characters and he is not interested in any of the major issues or burning social problems of the day. He does not describe, he does not explain; he suggests and leaves the reader to move along with him and draw his own but inevitable conclusions. He achieves actuality by writing all the time in the first person.

Roelants has published a collection of verse and much literary criticism, and was also a founder of a new Flemish literary review, *'t Fonteintje*, designed to follow in the tradition of *Van Nu En Straks* and to enhance still more the prestige of Flemish letters in the period between the wars. His creative prose writings consist of four novels, a few short plays and collections of short stories. Of these latter *De Jazz-speler* ('The Jazz Player', 1928) is the best known. His latest novel, *Gebed om een goed Einde* ('Prayer for a Good End', 1944) is largely autobiographical. *Komen en Gaan* ('Come and Go', 1927) is a masterpiece of psychological analysis. The remaining two novels are called respectively *Het Leven dat wij droomden* ('The Life We Dreamt', 1931) and *Alles komt terecht* ('Everything will come right', 1937).

4

In this present post-war period there are many Flemish novelists at work, and they all seem to have taken heart from the new vitality that followed on the efforts of the group *'t Fonteintje* ('The Little Spring') and that made its most noticeable impact in the early 1930's. It would be futile merely to catalogue their names, and if I select only two of the older generation for discussion here it is simply that they are the only two I have read, and that I read them because they were strongly recommended at the time of reading as both highly promising and 'curious'.

Johan DAISNE (1912–   ), again a native of Ghent, has produced several promising collections of verse, short stories, and two or three haunting novels which clearly indicate where his particular talents and genius lie. It is as a prose-writer, and as one with a marked Kafka-esque quality about him, that he is most likely to be remembered. For what the title is worth, he calls himself a 'magic-realist'. He is easily the most 'cerebral' and the most intellectual writer of his period, and yet all this is allied to a strong vein of romanticism and (at times) almost adolescent and masculine sentimentality and cynicism.

In *De Trap van Steen en Wolken* ('The Stairway of Stone and Clouds', 1942) Daisne is concerned with relating the life of reality and actuality with that of dreams – of constructing a stairway from the stones to the clouds that points the magic and only possible way to true happiness. His hero is made to project his everyday existence against that of his youth, to measure it against the past and against the possibilities for adventure that exist. His genius as a novelist in this book lies in his psychological insight and in the way in which he compels belief in every detail of the narrative as it unfolds itself.

De Man die zijn Haar kort liet knippen ('The Man who had his Hair Cut Short', 1947) is concerned with the plight of a man on the brink of insanity. No morbid detail is spared, and we are treated (if that is the word) to a deliberate and calm description of the autopsy of the hero's beloved – an autopsy in which all the morbid secrets of a fast decaying body are revealed. It is one long pulsating monologue, reminiscent of James Joyce for its juxtaposition of the most heterogeneous elements in one continual flow, and of Kafka because of the almost mathematical precision with which the nightmare detail is pinned down.

Louis-Paul Boon (1912–) is a writer with a social conscience, whose earlier novels were written very much under the influence of Walschap. He conceives of his task as novelist, however, in a somewhat different light from either Walschap or Roelants, or indeed any of his predecessors. He is interested neither in depicting the spiritual crises of his characters nor in discussing social or moral problems. He describes himself as a kind of seismograph recording as accurately as possible the pertur-bations about him. This in turn implies that he needs a giant canvas on which to work, and that his canvas will be peopled with a host of characters. It means that his novels are *romans-fleuves* and that they are lengthy and diffuse though never boring. It is Boon's particular talent and genius as a novelist that prevents this. He has very much the 'camera-eye' of Christopher Isherwood and he manages to pick out each of the many characters in his books, to seize hold of the striking and essential detail, to 'fix' it, and then to compel its being held in suspension in the reader's mind, as it were, until he is ready for the next move forward in which that particular character is concerned. All is grist that comes to Boon's mill, and he performs a kind of 'mass-observation' act. He does not hesitate to weave into his books stories of old revolutionaries and legends such as Reynard the Fox.

If he has a philosophy to preach it is that the world is awry. He depicts life's absurdities and its cruelties. Each sentence he writes is loaded with conflict, and he stands as a kind of impartial but shrewd observer and commentator on all that passes before his eye. His heroes are as numerous as the milling and jostling crowd and the reactions of his heroes are usually at the same primitive level. His style is that of the crowd, of the individuals composing the ugly motley about him, and he punctuates it with his own scoffing and surgical comments, much in the way of a Greek chorus. From this point of view he is, in many respects, reminiscent of the earlier Céline of the sprawling pre-war novels, *Voyage au bout de la Nuit* and *Mort à Crédit*.

His first published novel, *De Voorstad groeit* ('The Swarming Suburb', 1943), won him immediate attention and respect. There followed in rapid succession *Abel Gholaerts* (1944) and *Vergeten Straat* ('The Forgotten Street', 1945). *Mijn kleine Oorlog* ('My Little War', 1946) is easily the best war novel that has so far been published in Belgium and is written with deep intensity of feeling and expression. Latterly, Boon has evolved a still more personal and self-involved approach to novel-writing by placing himself as a kind of actor-commentator in his stories and holding his own conversations with the characters he depicts. Typical novels of this latter period are *De Kapellekensbaan* ('Chapel Street', 1953) and *Zomer te Ter-Muren* ('Summer in Ter-Muren', 1956).

One Belgian critic has somewhat disparagingly decried Boon as writing 'rancorous, grumbling books . . . filled with the shouts and scoffing of a teeming, restless and unimportant multitude.' Fleming though the critic is, and probably more competent to judge work in his native tongue than I can be, I feel that he is being both unjust and limited in his approach to Boon's work. Boon is a sincere novelist, a most industrious novelist of great ability. He is deeply concerned about the future of Flemish letters and convinced with Vermeylen that to be a good Fleming is the first step to becoming a good European. He seeks the unity through diversity preached by the founders of *Van Nu En Straks*. He strives to uphold the dignity of man by highlighting his present despair. Conscientiously he relates his art to the whole of life.

CHAPTER SEVEN

The Modern Novel in French

I

THE EXHILARATING tussles between the leading literary reviews of French expression that we have described in some detail in Chapter Two had interesting and un-expected results as far as the development of the novel as an art form was concerned. The leading Flemish periodical, *Van Nu En Straks*, it will be remembered, had as its main objective that of raising the cultural life and standards of the whole Flemish people. It was frankly propagandist, and it was severely practical and undeviating in pursuit of its objective. It rightly revered Flanders' one great and popular poet, Guido Gezelle, but it failed to produce anyone else approaching his calibre. The novel and the short story became the popular art form. Literary reviews of French expression were concerned solely with art for art's sake. *La Jeune Belgique*, even in its earliest days, had paid scant heed to Edmond Picard's theories of the social purpose of the artist. Edmond Picard in turn soon neglected his avowed further aim of creating a truly national literary revival and was by 1886 devoting issue after issue of *L'Art Moderne* to the new Symbolist writers and decrying as old-fashioned the Parnassian approach of *La Jeune Belgique*. True, Albert Mockel's *La Wallonie* owed its birth to that tempestuous young man's dismay at the creation of a Flemish Academy of Letters and his consequent resolve to relate Walloon culture to the main streams of French literary activity. That phase, however, soon passed into one in which, having opened the pages of *La Wallonie* to the dis-possessed French Symbolist writers, he turned his review into the leading Symbolist publication throughout Europe.

In other words, the editors of these various reviews of French expression were first and foremost passionately interested in literature and paid only convenient lip-service to their Belgian heritage. That does not mean that they were not good patriots. It does mean, though, that they put their art first and that they felt (however obscurely) that to prostitute or circumscribe their art in any way amounted to a betrayal both of themselves and their heritage. They encouraged every young Belgian writer of promise who wrote in French. The source of his inspiration, whether it was his native Ghent, Antwerp, the Campine, the Ardennes, was of no importance. What became of importance was (*a*) that the educated Fleming had been educated in the French tongue and therefore became, as an artist and writer, of French expression rather than of Flemish, and (*b*) that his native genius was perfectly attuned to the modern symbolist approach. French-speaking Flemings such as Maeterlinck, Verhaeren, Van Lerberghe, Grégoire Le Roy, set the pace and their Walloon compatriots followed after. What was of equal importance was that the novel as an art form was in consequence neglected in favour of poetry and drama.

Thus, after Camille Lemonnier and Georges Eekhoud we have first to content ourselves, as far as fiction is concerned, with the small-scale and regionalist writings of Louis Delattre, Marie Gevers and Jean Tousseul. Charming though they may be in their own quiet reaches, they hardly enter the mainstream of European literature. We have to wait until 1920 before that admirable *pointilliste* and pathetic original, André Baillon, astounds us with *Moi, Quelque Part* and in the last twelve feverish years of his life gives us an equal number of exciting works. We have also to wait until the 1920's for the genius of Franz Hellens as a novelist to assert itself. Note that both these writers are of Flemish extraction and that Hellens is a considerable if not a major poet. The first outstanding and pure Walloon writer to emerge in the inter-wars years, and, incidentally, the first Belgian to win the *Prix Goncourt*, was Charles Plisnier. He also began as a poet and has acquired a high reputation as such.

Dissimilar as these three major novelists are in outlook, temperament and choice of subject, they have one important thing in common. They are universal as opposed to regionalist writers. It was presumably his strong feelings about the necessity for universality in the artist that led Hellens to gather around him Plisnier, Marie Gevers, Grégoire Le Roy, Robert Vivier and a number of younger writers in his *groupe du lundi* and to utter the now famous 1937 declaration of his group that condemned in no uncertain terms particularism and the idea of a national literature. With Hellens as its chief spokesman the group claimed that the 'Soyons nous-mêmes' motto of *La Jeune Belgique* had been unfortunate in that it had led to a kind of regionalistic writing that was keeping Belgian literary effort out of the main streams of European thought. The first important task of the new writers, therefore, was to make a clean break with regionalism.

Generally speaking, present-day writers have tended to take notice of this manifesto, and I am afraid the result has been not exactly what Hellens and his group desired. Once again it has led to neglect of the novel in favour of poetry and drama and belles-lettres. The only authors of present note are Pierre Nothomb, who escapes the charge of regionalism by his own carefully peopled never-never land; Robert Vivier, who usually takes a recognizable provincial (Belgian) setting to work out a universal problem and allows the lambency of his own poetic genius to illuminate the whole; Anne-Marie Bodart and her husband Roger Bodart (primarily a poet) – their technique in this sense is not dissimilar from that of Vivier, but Bodart is an essayist of charm and felicity and not a novelist; Adrien Jans, who has no truck at all with the Hellens manifesto and is un-ashamedly regionalist; and Francis Walder, the professional soldier turned writer, who, for the novel that won him the 1958 *Prix Goncourt*, had the happy inspiration of drawing on his un-rivalled knowledge of twentieth-century international round-table conferences to reconstruct the scene at Saint-Germain-en-Laye which led to the 1570 Peace of Saint-Germain.

Then, of course, there is the incomparable Georges Simenon and his French Inspector of Police, Maigret. But how French exactly is Maigret? And how Parisian Maigret's Paris and how French the French provincial cities where crime takes Maigret on occasions? I have the naughty impression that the average Belgian would feel more at home than the Frenchman in the settings Simenon devises, and more at home in conversation and beer drinking (and pipe-smoking) with Maigret. . . .

2

Louis DELATTRE (1870–1938) is a regionalist of great charm and simplicity and on this account probably one of the best of Belgian short-story writers. He never strives for effect. He knows his own limitations and severely disciplines himself to describe only the people and scenery of his native province of Hainaut and in particular of his own village of Fontaine-l'Evêque. He trained as a doctor and he came back to his own people to serve them and minutely and lovingly to observe and comment on their simple joys and their everyday pains, pleasures and tribulations. He is filled with pity and love for the courage of the humble working class and for their rude and practical philosophy of life. He loves children and animals without becoming senti-mental about them. In a very few words he can bring a scene vividly to life, animate it and also point his moral. Thus, in one unforgettable picture of the aged roast-chestnut seller with her pitch at the corner of a draughty street in the middle of winter he tells us:

C'est grande fête, demain. C'est Noël. Les sous sortent facilement des poches. Les pauvres eux-mêmes trouvent quelques vieux liards couverts de vert de gris pour goûter à la pulpe fumante des châtaignes craquantes. La marchande de la rue est heureuse de tenir la boutique du feu. Les mains roulées dans son tablier, elle piétine sur place, se dandine, chantonne, fait claquer ses sabots sur les dalles. Son visage fripé étincelle comme une pomme rouge et ratatinée, sous les replis de son châle de laine . . .

Son nez goutte . . . Et elle agite la tête au rythme du bime-bame de bronze. (Of the church bells now ringing.)

'Chauds, chauds, les marrons!'

Il lui semble à chaque cri qu'elle pousse, que non sa voix seule, mais toute elle-même, parcourt et couvre au galop la place autour d'elle. Comme elle attise le feu du réchaud et retourne à pleines mains sur la tôle les marrons qui rougissent et crépitent! De sa grande fourchette de fer elle frappe sur le lourd couvercle comme sur une joyeuse cymbale . . . Voilà! Elle fait son pauvre

métier ainsi qu'une autre danserait. Elle crie ses marrons à
vendre comme une autre chanterait. Il y a dans ses mouvements
une fièvre d'ardeur: et c'est la joie.

In all, Delattre published between 1891 and 1911 seven
different volumes of short stories dealing with life in his native
village, with recollections of his own childhood and student days,
and with poignant incidents in the lives of those who were his
patients and his friends. His best work is generally considered to
be *Une Rose à la Bouche* (1896), *Le Roman du Chien et de l'Enfant*
(1907), *Les Carnets d'un Médecin de Campagne* (1910), and *Le
Parfum des Buis* (1911), from which the above extract is taken.

Marie GEVERS (1883–) was once epitomized in one of
Albert Mockel's picturesque phrases as 'un cœur qui a des
yeux'. One can see what he means. Though primarily a poet, she
has written short stories, travel stories and novels which, like her
poetry, speak the whole time of the magic of just being alive. In
one of her first novels, *La Comtesse des Digues* (1931), she makes her
heroine, Suzanne, say that her father taught her to read and to
write, to love the water, the earth and the wind, and this in effect
sums up the whole of Marie Gevers's own existence. Except for a
short stay in the Belgian Congo she has rarely left her native
Campine and Polder district near Antwerp and along the wind-
swept shores of the river Scheldt. All her life as woman, mother
and writer she has remained close to and in almost sensual
contact with nature and in love principally with trees, wind and
water. In one sense she is a 'romancière du bonheur'; in another
an avowed pantheist; in still another a kind of 'Colette du nord'.
I must confess that much as I admire Colette as a stylist I am
somewhat repelled by this sensuous process of self-identification
with nature. The same holds true for Marie Gevers and I
infinitely prefer her poetry to her prose works. In any case she
started as a poet.

Madame Orpha ou la Sérénade de Mai (1934), which followed on
the well-merited success of *La Comtesse de Digues*, was popular in
almost the novelette sense by the smooth insinuation of a plot of
pure adultery as an almost secondary theme into a main story of
early-summer nature festivities. *Guldentop* (1935) retells the
macabre and popular folk tale of a brigand who, decapitated, is

the terror of the Campine villages he once knew. *La Ligne de Vie* (1937), *Paix sur les Champs* (1941) and *La Grande Marée* (1943) represent the best of Marie Gevers in the earlier vein.

The passionate attachment of Marie Gevers to the Campine is matched in a different but no less fervent manner by that of Jean TOUSSEUL (1890–1944) to the valley of the Meuse and particularly to his birthplace, Landenne-sur-Meuse. His most vivid recollections are of early childhood spent in this rural retreat. His own life, however, was not an easy one. His health was far from robust, his parents were poor and his education was in consequence curtailed. By the age of twenty-one he was an ordinary, unskilled quarry-worker. Patiently, and in his scant spare time, he continued for himself his interrupted education. He read widely and came particularly under the influence of the Russian writers Tolstoy and Dostoevsky and of that great humanist, Romain-Rolland.

Journalistic work during World War I and the publication of a series of sketches and recollections of his early days at Landenne proved a happy apprenticeship for his one, long major work, a *roman-fleuve* strongly influenced by Romain-Rolland's *Jean-Christophe* and entitled *Jean Clarambaux*. The first volume, *Le Village Gris*, appeared in 1927. There then followed *Le Retour* (1930), *L'Eclaircie* (1931), *La Rafale* (1933) and *Le Testament* (1936).

The main interest of *Jean Clarambaux*, which is for the most part autobiographical, lies in the way in which Tousseul manages to convey the sensitive yet cantankerous nature of his hero; his generosity amid all his suffering; his feelings of aloneness yet of oneness with others of the same humble origins; the loves, passions and superstitions of those about him; their inescapable identification with the countryside in which they live and with the jobs they must do. Tousseul is an unequal writer, but at its best his prose has a firmness and an hallucinatory simplicity and economy about it that manages to convey just the emotion the author has so sincerely experienced. Thus, in describing a summer's evening he can write:

Les campagnes arrondies sentaient le blé mûr. Le matin, elles fumaient un peu et le soleil les laissait tout humides jusqu'à midi. Un flamboiement poudré d'or vibrait pendant des heures sous la coupe bleue de l'horizon. On ne voyait plus personne. Mais lorsque l'astre devenait rouge comme un gros fruit vermeil et qu'il musait le long des collines, les éteules apparaissaient nues, les terres retournées prenaient une bonne odeur concentrée, les chemins couraient allègrement avec des lacets tentants le long des pignons purs qui buvaient tout ce qui restait de clarté autour d'eux et les petites gens, menus, aigus, remuaient dans la douceur de soir: on eût dit qu'ils venaient de sortir du sol. Le ciel changeait à chaque minute; une ligne blanche cernait les silhouettes des collines et des maisons et tremblait autour d'elles, comme un filet d'eau. Un peu de fumée montait d'une cheminée, violette et droite. De gros oiseaux couraient puis s'envolaient au ras du sol avec un bruit de moteur.

Il faisait doux. La campagne se recueillait comme le bois, après avoir offert son flanc fécond au baiser ardent de la journée.

3

To turn from the kind of personal novel that Tousseul gives us and to pick up any one novel of André BAILLON (1875–1932) is to leave the pleasing and attractive shallows of everyday existence and to plumb for the first time since Camille Lemonnier the anguish, perplexities, hopes and aspirations of real living. Baillon is as much a personal novelist as is Tousseul. In the narrow sense he is also a regionalist. With Baillon, however, regionalism is but an excuse for writing, a means to an end only, and that end can best be described as an attempt to exteriorize the human situation. Gide attempted it in his personal novels. So did Stendhal. And like Stendhal, Baillon aims not so much at being himself as at being like nobody else. Again like Stendhal, Baillon attaches great importance to precise and detailed analysis of a state of mind and to illustrating this state of mind by an accumulation of convincing and detailed evidence. Like Stendhal, he is simple and direct in his approach, distrusts the conventional, and avoids any flow of rhetoric. Like Mérimée, he invents nothing, and like Balzac he shows up the ugly side to man's life and the influences contributing thereto. Materialistic like Zola, he totally lacks Zola's pessimism. He is not a romantic. He is not a realist. He is an impressionist with a strong vein of Flemish mysticism. And like the Goncourt brothers he carefully notes those details of everyday existence which tomorrow or the day after would otherwise have been lost. All his writing is one long flood of self-confession in which sentiment and cynicism, irony and humour, penetrating observation and a tender compassionate lyricism all play their part. He has a profound knowledge of human nature, an uncanny understanding of *scrupules de conscience* and of the passions that make wreck of a man's soul as well as torture his body.

In *Histoire d'une Marie* (1921) he says of his heroine:

Marie était douillette des reins et de cœur sensible. Elle avait 22 ans, une jolie taille svelte, une peau soyeuse d'un blanc lumineux. Il ne manquait à ses joues qu'un peu de rose et de chair. Ses yeux riaient doux. Mais quand elle pleurait, ses lèvres semblaient arracher un baiser, toujours prêt à tomber.

He is particularly skilful in making convincing a kind of interior soliloquy when the character, confident that there is no eavesdropper, permits himself to voice aloud for his own cold comfort his real feelings. Thus the mother of Marie, as she watches her daughter leaving home, bursts out:

Petite Marie, toi qui m'a gonflé les flancs; toi, dont je pressais avec espoir les lèvres contre mes mamelles; toi, dont j'aimais découvrir au berceau les jambes joyeuses et les menottes vers moi tendues . . . ma chair encore une fois s'ouvre et saigne à cause de toi. Je t'ai donné mon sang, mon lait, mes fatigues, ma vie. . . . Tu t'en vas, et j'ai peur. . . .

And Baillon adds:

Elle pensait cela, la pauvre mère, et d'autres choses encore, plus confuses.

In *Le Neveu de Mademoiselle Autorité* (1930) he writes of his hero (himself):

Je n'ignore pas ce que je suis. Un roseau. De la vase comme nourriture; des coups de vent pour le dehors. Peu de chose. C'est de ce roseau qu'il s'agira: le roseau-moi, les roseaux-eux, car vit-on jamais roseau pousser seul? . . . .

Or again in *Histoire d'une Marie*:

Il aimait rire, mais cela ne se voyait pas; il riait à l'intérieur, il riait triste. . . .

On veut écrire, et vite. On porte en soi des rêves, des mots, des idées, peut-être d'anciennes souffrances, peut-être des espoirs frais. Souffrances et espoirs, on veut montrer tout cela . . . Oui, mais la phrase qui hésite! Les mots sont des oiseaux qui n'éclosent pas comme des poules au bout de trois semaines. Il faut des mois, il faut des ans, il faut, pour les couver, la poitrine tiède de la douleur . . . ou peut-être le chaud de la joie . . . ou peut-être . . . On a 25 ans, on ne sait pas, on cherche.

André Baillon was 45 and not 25 years of age when he published his first novel, *Moi, Quelque Part* (re-issued in 1922 with the title of *En Sabots*). It was composed in his dark and tiny Brussels flat during the difficult days of German occupation and represents the highly successful attempt of an already harassed and neurasthenic man to recapture the peace, calm and serenity of mind that had been his during two separate visits (well before the war) to the tiny Flemish village of Westmalle. There he had humbly identified himself with the simple villagers and shared their most menial tasks. There he had run a poultry farm and shared the simplest of cottages with his extraordinary wife (the Marie of the novel) who had to be mother to him as well and who also, if the truth be told, was probably happiest with him at Westmalle. There he had found solace in the company of Trappists from a nearby monastery and had even thought of joining the order. There he had decided to put all literary ambition firmly behind him.

The success of *Moi, Quelque Part* finally decided him to abandon his secure but frustrating job on the editorial staff of the newspaper *La Dernière Heure* (to be the subject of another novel, *Par Fil Spécial*, published in 1924) and to go to Paris to launch himself as an author. The faithful 'Marie' accompanied him, found she had to share him with Germaine Lievens whom he had met in 1913 and with whom he had spent most of the war years, and not unnaturally soon returned to Belgium. Despite the encouragement of Germaine Lievens, he found it difficult to make a living as a writer. His neurasthenia increased and in 1923 he spent several months in *La Salpêtrière* (a famous mental hospital). There 'Marie' visited him for the last time. He was back in Salpêtrière again in 1925. In 1931 he attempted to commit suicide. A second suicide attempt on 7 April 1932 led to his death three days later.

None the less, these twelve hectic and unhappy years in Paris were years of great literary activity. In 1921 he published *Histoire d'une Marie*, in which he told how the lonely, intro- spective young man of 25 answered an advertisement the prostitute 'Marie' inserted in a matrimonial journal, *Le Flirt*, and so found himself a wife and a mother-figure:

> Il était maigre, il était frêle: il avait quelque chose d'un petit enfant . . . ses cheveux sur ses oreilles pendaient comme des oreilles tristes de caniche. Vraiment un drôle de petit bon- homme. . . .

> Marie, tu es ma maîtresse, mais aussi tu seras beaucoup ma maman. J'étais trop jeune quand j'avais une maman.

The purely autobiographical run of stories is then broken for a time to give us a straightforward novel of prostitution, *Zonzon Pépette, Fille de Londres* (1923), the newspaper novel mentioned above, and then the poignant sketches of life and states of mind in a mental institution: *Un Homme si Simple* (1925), *Chalet I* (1926), *Délires* (1927), *La Vie est Quotidienne* (1929). In the last years of his life he picked up the thread of autobiography. *Histoire d'une Marie* and *Moi, Quelque Part* had told his life story from 1900 to the war years. The remaining novels, published in no definite chronological order, fill in the earlier part. They are: *Le Perce- Oreille du Luxembourg* (1928), *Le Neveu de Mademoiselle Autorité* (1930), *Le Roseau* (1932) and *La Dupe* published posthumously in 1944.

It is an extraordinary story André Baillon has to tell, a story that fully matches his betrothal of 'Marie' and a story that in the telling has to run the whole gamut of human suffering and experience. Disentangling fact from fiction we learn that André Baillon was of lower-middle-class parentage and was born in Antwerp in 1875, the youngest of four boys. His eldest brother died of meningitis when quite young. The other two brothers became respectively a lawyer and a priest and had little time to spare for their wayward and unorthodox sibling. André's father died when he was only a month old. His mother married again but died herself when André was still only five years old. No wonder that in *Le Neveu de Mademoiselle Autorité* Baillon writes:

> Si je faisais de la littérature je décrirais les cloches qui sonnent, l'oncle Jacques en deuil, moi qui pleure, ces horribles cor- billards anversois tout peints en or, avec des tombes, des saules pleureurs, des Pierrot-le-Mort un peu partout. En vérité je ne me souviens que d'une chose. J'avais ma petite expérience des enterrements.

The maternal grandparents wrested the gentle and with- drawn child from his step-father and did their best for him:

> Je voudrais vous présenter un tas de braves gens qui étaient mes parents de Termonde et je ne sais vraiment trop comment m'y prendre.

Between 1883 and 1889 he was at school with the Jesuits at Turnhout ('Quand les Jésuites vous ont bourré de Dieu, un jour on y croit, un autre pas') and then was ignominiously expelled, a scapegoat and innocent victim of homosexual practices. From 1889 to 1893 he was at the Catholic College of Louvain. He then started studying to become a civil engineer but abandoned his studies for a liaison with a servant girl, Rosa (1894–1898), who cheated the young innocent of all his money. He finally drifted to Brussels with the vague intention of becoming a writer. The response he made from the depths of his loneliness to 'Marie's' own *cri de cœur* secured him some fourteen years of security and happy companionship with the large-hearted but simple, un- lettered and uncomplicated heroine of his first two novels.

Properly speaking, however, there is neither a hero nor a heroine to any of Baillon's novels. It is more a question, as he put it in his own trenchant way, of 'le roseau-moi et les roseaux-eux'. He tries to be himself; he lets 'Marie' be herself; he peoples his canvas with a number of other selves and shows us how the most ordinary and humdrum of people in the most humdrum existence can have adventures and emotions completely un-suspected. He himself figures as a kind of lay saint who sacrifices position, hopes of fame and reputation to rescue from oblivion, and with all their faults and prejudices, a handful of ordinary saint-sinners like himself who lack his perspicacity and gift of speech. It has quite rightly been stated that Baillon owes much to Jules Renard for the composition of *Moi, Quelque Part*. Renard's influence is hardly in evidence in the other works. What André Baillon has done has been to anticipate Sartre by showing man throwing himself into the world, suffering there, wrestling there, and so bit by bit defining himself and creating his own being. It is no mean achievement.

4

Though in every respect different from Baillon, Franz HELLENS (1881–) is in one sense complementary to him. Baillon introduces a newer realism into the novel and stems directly from Camille Lemonnier and Georges Eekhoud. Franz Hellens follows the symbolist tradition and wrests reality from men's dreams and hallucinations. For Hellens the fantastic and the real are inseparable and we may only reach for what is real through the fantastic. 'La vraie vie est celle du rêve,' he writes in *Mélusine*. Like Maeterlinck, Verhaeren, Van Lerberghe and Grégoire Le Roy, Franz Hellens was a pupil of the Collège Sainte-Barbe in Ghent. Like them he is of pure Flemish ex-traction and from the well-to-do middle class. He is also the last of this group of writers (*les déracinés* as he puts it) to receive in Ghent a purely French upbringing and education.

As Hellens has since confessed to Roger Bodart, however, he feels and acts as a genuine *deraciné*, and this feeling of having his roots firmly in Flanders and his intellectual existence in the pure

French tradition probably provides the key to his surrealist technique. At the age of eighteen (so he again tells us) he fell under the spell of Edgar Allan Poe, recognized Poe's mastery of an exciting and essentially new technique, but gradually came to reverse his master's procedure:

> Le rôle de l'écrivain me paraît consister à intégrer le réel dans l'imaginaire. Je ne construis pas, comme Poë, des histoires dont tous les rouages sont prévus et contrôlés . . . Alors que Poë procède de l'inconnu au connu, du fantastique au réel, je prends au contraire mon élan de la réalité pour aboutir au fantastique . . . Procédant de la sorte de l'extérieur à l'intérieur, du concret à l'abstrait, je rencontre le mystère sans le chercher, et au lieu de poser le problème en commençant, je termine par une interrogation et n'explique rien.

All Franz Hellens's earlier work shows him broodingly pre-occupied with and haunted by sights, sounds and impressions of his adoptive city, Ghent, which he describes as 'aimée entre toutes comme une maîtresse jalouse'. He is fascinated by the medieval past as it impinges on the present; by the corroded stonework of wall, castle, church and turret; by the hovels; by the religious obsessions, again of a medieval kind, of the devout of all classes who turn the city into a kind of 'visage de ville penché sur une croix, hanté de médisance et d'obsécration et qui semble porter une dérisoire couronne d'épines'. His first novel, *En Ville Morte* (1906), is very much in the traditional regionalist trend of Eekhoud, but – and this is important as an indication of the direction in which Hellens's genius was already turning – it bears the sub-title of 'Ville Morte aux néfastes ruelles, terrassée par l'ombre tyrannique du monstre médiéval'. Two collections of short stories which then followed – *Les Hors-le-Vent* (1909) and *Les Clartés Latentes: vingt contes et paraboles* (1912) – emphasized the parable effect he was seeking, and the former work moved the discerning Edmond Picard to declare that with Hellens we had 'la naissance d'un talent nouveau où le fantastique et le réel, tantôt s'équilibrent, tantôt se disputent à la manière de certains primitifs flamands, sans que l'un de ces éléments parviennent à dominer l'autre'.

Hellens's third collection of short stories, *Nocturnal, précédé de quinze histoires*, was published in 1919. Here for the first time he completely liberates himself from his regionalistic phase and finds himself in terms of the earlier prophecy uttered by Picard. *Nocturnal* is little more than a narration of a series of dreams the author had between 1 October 1918, and 13 January 1919, and the fifteen stories preceding this unusual documentary herald his theory of *réalité fantastique*. Each story is carefully built up from a series of detailed and prosaic events to lead inevitably to the fantastic and inexplicable. 'La Courge' is a typical, and perhaps the best, example. The author, dining with a banker friend after attending the funeral of an unnamed person, is told by the banker that he at least knows what happens to us after death. He has come into possession of a curious gourd, shaped as a water-bottle, and contemplation of this object has on repeated occasions introduced a dream state in which he is compelled to retrace all stages of his previous existences on earth. The banker concludes the narration, as the author concludes his story, with the words:

> Voilà. Ne riez pas. Je sens, je suis convaincu que je fus moine et ermite, quelque part, sous le soleil, avant d'être banquier. J'ignore sous quelle forme je reparaîtrai ailleurs après cette vie. Mais je sais qu'une suite d'existences diverses m'attendent encore au sortir de celle-ci. Il est regrettable que tous les hommes qui pensent et s'inquiètent ne reçoivent pas comme moi quelque courge pour leur révéler ce que la réflexion et toute la philosophie du monde ne pourront jamais leur apprendre.

World War I was decisive in the career of Franz Hellens in that it forced him to leave the circumscribing atmosphere of his native Flanders and seek what became for him the magical and mystical light of Provence and the south of France. So far, characteristically, he had travelled only in England, Germany, Austria and Poland. He now settled for a long time in southern France, in Nice, where he met his wife and where he became passionately interested in problems of literature and of modern art. There, during the years 1917–1918, he composed his master-piece *Mélusine* (1920), a novel which, he tells us, 'fut écrit littérale-ment dans un état de transe où je fus plongé pendant toute une période d'étrange fécondité . . . Je n'ai jamais rêvé autant que pendant cette période de seize mois environ, où les chapitres de *Mélusine* furent écrits sous cette mystérieuse dictée.'

Thus, long before the popularization of Freud's theories on dreams in either France or Belgium, and before the surrealists had discovered for themselves the virtues of the technique of dream inspiration, Hellens had forged for himself with *Nocturnal* and *Mélusine* his own and peculiar type of literary creation. And from 1920 onwards we have had a steady and almost annual output of prose writings in which the sternly factual and the equally compulsive fantastic intermingle, coalesce, and sometimes pursue their separate paths the better to work that peculiar process of alchemy by which Hellens seeks to free his reader from the oppressive and fallacious certainties of modern materialistic existence.

In *Mélusine* Hellens plays havoc with legendary and mythical figures, invents a new kind of Merlin (Nilrem), and sometimes inextricably mixes Nilrem with his own admired modern mythical figure, Charlie Chaplin, who bears the endearing name of Locharlochi. Indeed, the whole story is conceived in terms of the cinematographic technique of Chaplin in his heyday. As the book opens we are in the middle of the Sahara, and the hero, accompanied by Mélusine, is about to visit a huge cathedral with neither doors nor windows and built entirely of a kind of translucent material. Within the cathedral, piloted by Nilrem, they explore an extraordinary new world and visit a vast hall filled with machines of all kinds, machines designed to replace the worn-out mythologies of the gods:

Autrefois les hommes allaient d'un pas traînant, mal avisé, ou se contentaient de piétiner. Ils adoraient l'eau, le feu, le vent, ils inventèrent les dieux. Les dieux sont morts. Nos maîtres, nous les avons créés nous-mêmes dans les machines.

Their guide through the machine shop is a curiously comically dressed creature, a kind of clown in modern dress who reveals himself as Locharlochi and who explains at some length why he is as he is:

La raison de mon habillement et de certains gestes qui vous font rire est fort simple. Pour enseigner mes contemporains je me suis

fait comédien. Notre époque réclame des prouesses, elle exige de
l'adresse sous une apparence grotesque et malhabile. . . . Je
parais. Tout le monde rit. On me croit gauche et maladroit, je
me heurte aux objets, je trébuche, me relève. A travers le rire
l'étonnement commence à percer. On me suit. Je déploie mes
souplesses. Chaque passe est applaudie. Je produis en même
temps la vitesse et le rire. En vingt secondes, j'ai parcouru tout le
chemin et propagé une multiple gaîté. On ne sait plus si l'on a ri
davantage ou admiré. Mais le rire que j'éveille est aussi éloigné
de celui des dieux d'Homère que l'auto de Pierpont Morgan
diffère du char d'Hector. C'est le rire bref, sec, amer, saccadé et
détonnant d'une époque affairée, le trépignement d'une
humanité positive et désabusée.

Bass-Bassina-Boulou (1922) betrays Hellens's preoccupation
with African art and sorcery and tells the odyssey of a simple
wooden idol which, from primitive and exciting beginnings,
finishes up as a collector's item, is stolen and sold to a Negro
barman, finds its way to a junk shop, is thrown into the street by a
capricious child and finally perishes in the furnaces of the town's
scavenging department. The style is clear, direct and simple and
matches the sincerity of purpose with which the author, obviously
and yet with reverent restraint, is symbolizing both the *adventures*
of Christ to His death and resurrection and the rise and decline
of the Christian faith to modern times.

With *Bass-Bassina-Boulou*, *Réalités Fantastiques* (1923) and *Œil-
de-Dieu* (1925), Hellens completes his period of apprenticeship
to his own chosen form of expression, deploys his cult of the
fantastic to the full to test all its possibilities and limitations to
depict stark reality and strip reality of its own particular frenzy,
and gradually perfects his own dry, rapid and nervous style that
so particularly suits his approach and carries with it complete
conviction. His dream-state voyages of exploration come full
circle and focus finally on the dreamer. The publication of *Le
Naïf* in 1926 heralds a series of novels – *Les Filles du Désir* (1930),
Frédéric (1935), *Le Magasin aux Poudres* (1936), *Naître et Mourir*
(1948), *L'Homme de Soixante Ans* (1951), *Les Marées de l'Escaut*
(1953), *Les Saisons de Pontoise* (1956) – in which he draws on his
own clear analysis of childhood and adolescence and depicts
himself or his heroes (his other-selves) as they are. All possible

changes of mood are caught and held pregnant with meaning. There is no 'emotion recollected in tranquillity' but rather a stirring of tranquillity. Again and again he is at pains to show that both persons and things have several faces and that the real truth – the truth that matters – lies far beyond mere sense intuition.

To try to illustrate the mature Hellens's method is almost impossible in a short quotation, for all depends on cumulative effect. We can make some attempt, however, with the episode 'Le Gâteau du Dimanche' taken from *Frédéric*. Frédéric, the hero of the story, is a young boy who delights in daily games in his father's large garden. He is preoccupied by the changing seasons of the year – in his healthy, animal state almost unknowingly preoccupied. Trees die and are cut down. Branches are lopped to make other trees more sturdy and shapely. Fruits come to harvest. Eggs are hatched and young ducklings comically herald the recurring miracle of creation. But Frédéric's father is a doctor. One Sunday Frédéric's happy rhythmic existence is troubled slightly by the necessity for acknowledging the unrhythmic impingement of human suffering. The local pastry-cook brings her consumptive daughter for treatment:

> Un dimanche, une phtisique traversa le jardin pour venir consulter mon père.
>
> Les arbres et les bêtes en parurent contrariés. Tout ce qui vivait et poussait, voisinant la mort, détestait la faiblesse et la maladie. Une plante qui déclinait, nous l'achevions sans pitié. Le gros arbre écrasait le petit. Parfois des chênes jumeaux se disputaient l'air et la lumière; si l'un d'eux dépérissait, Bernard arrivait avec sa cognée, comme si le plus fort l'eût appelé.
>
> La santé et la mort étaient seules admises dans ce monde dont nous étions les maîtres.

But this shadow cast across the existence of Frédéric by the presence in the garden of an ailing child who is neither living nor dead is compensated for by the weekly gift from the grateful pastry-cook of a magnificent cake that is eaten after dinner for dessert. Each week the cake is an excitingly different one.

Frédéric looks forward, not to the visit but to the arrival of the cake with apprehension, for each week the boy's father announces to his family that the girl cannot live much longer. When will she die and when will the cakes stop arriving?

Ce fut le dernier dimanche de septembre. Pour la première fois j'avais oublié de guetter l'arrivée de la phtisique. La cloche du déjeuner s'agita dans le vide.

Un grand trou était ouvert au milieu de la table où s'élevait d'habitude le gâteau.

– C'est un bienfait que Dieu l'ait reprise! dit ma mère.

Bernard avait abattu un hêtre qui se mourait depuis des mois.

The girl is dead. Her mother has not brought the cake. The following Sunday, however, all is well. The cake reappears. The grateful pastry-cook remembers the little boy. All is well again because the established pattern has reasserted itself, and more abundantly:

Le chemin de l'allée fut nettoyé par la pluie, le jardinier y passa le râteau. La semaine bondit plus fort et le dimanche parut sortir d'un long engourdissement. Un gâteau était reparu sur la table, orné de fruits confits.

However, the most astonishing production of Hellens in his maturity – astonishing because so unpredictable and so intensely aggressive – has proved to be *Moreldieu* (1946). Is the book the result of his brooding and dreaming during the agonizing hours of torture and cruelty and man's beastliness to man during the Second World War? Or is it a final release of pent-up emotions that could find no real outlet in his other works? Whatever the cause, Morel is the most sordid and unforgettable character that Hellens has given us. He is a disgusting and fascinating creature, repulsive and yet magnetic in his viciousness. One thinks immediately of Thomas Mann's *Felix Krull*, but Felix Krull is a rogue with charm, depicted with endearing irony. Morel is void of all moral worth, a vicious impostor who really comes to life, as it were, within the pages of the book and forces us to share with him all the turpitude and horror of his *saison en enfer*. We are not purged by going through the fire. We are only made more acutely and sickeningly aware of our own inescapable frailties.

Marcel Morel, the hero of the story, is a completely amoral person whose sole ambition is to be the equal of God. To this end he humiliates and betrays his best friends who might have saved him. He abuses all that is noble and pure. Instead of praising and building to man's greater glory he sullies, destroys and debases all man's good works. In one unforgettable scene of drunken orgy he has a vision of himself as he really is:

> Adieu, Morel! Tu retombes, tu n'es ni humble, ni modeste, tu n'as aucune personnalité, aucun tempérament. . . . C'est à Dieu que j'en veux! Je lui ai pris tout ce qu'il m'a refusé, tout ce qui m'appartenait et qu'on a écrasé dans mes doigts comme un raisin trop doux, pour ne laisser que l'aigre qui fait les rebelles. Je suis damné sur terre, repoussé, haï, laid, déformé. . . . Nous nous sommes mesurés, toi et moi, tu avais ta foudre et moi mon audace, toi le soleil et moi l'ivresse qui conduit à sa lumière. . . . Peut-être es-tu tout puissant, mais l'être que tu as créé a surpris ton secret. Tu n'as pas tout prévu; si le ciel est réservé aux esclaves, l'enfer, qui est aux forts, conduit aux mêmes altitudes. Ainsi disparaît tout mensonge.
>
> Un seul être au monde, un seul, aurait pu me sauver. C'est de lui qu'est venu tout le mal. Oui, le mal existe, il est beau, ton cadeau, Dieu immortel! Du reste, je n'en ai jamais voulu, il m'a été imposé. C'est pour cela que je t'ai nié, que je te nie encore. Un seul être au monde. A peine commençais-je à vivre. Je le hais. Je le hais. Ceci sera mon dernier mot. Je vous hais, sein maternel qui m'avez enfanté, lait maternel qui m'avez donné dès le berceau le goût de l'amer, terre maternelle où je vais rentrer, je vous hais, je n'ai jamais cessé de vous haïr. Ce n'est pas un homme, c'est un ver que vous avez nourri. J'ai ravagé toutes les innocences, dévoré tous les cœurs . . . Je me rongerai moi-même pour me prouver que j'existe et que je m'appartiens!

The parable effect is once again clear. Throughout all his writing Hellens has remained faithful to his own vision of the world and has patiently disciplined himself faithfully to convey to his reader his own state of mind. He is the poet turned novelist. Rarely does he describe an event or a situation; he prefers to record the impact such an event has made on him and to communicate to the reader the emotional and intellectual reaction. He is in this sense the prophet and seer that Victor Hugo fondly imagined himself to be, a modern Merlin, a psychologist preoccupied with human frailties who tries to understand and make us understand through the medium of his art. He does not explain; that is not his province. And as for the duality of his approach – the fantastic realities – is it really a duality? Is what *we* describe as the fantastic not a kind of hyper-realism? Does he not grasp reality, with his poet's vision, more surely than us and so apprehend more clearly the fantastic as the logical and inescapable prolongation of modern man's frenzy? Finally, if we must look for influences on Franz Hellens's work, we should remember that he began his long literary career when Maeterlinck was at the height of his fame as *the* Symbolist writer and Georges Eekhoud was acclaimed as the outstanding Belgian realist and regionalist. If his work is to be considered in some measure as a kind of synthesis of these two approaches it is also a synthesis in which he has resolutely tried to strip from both approaches their imperfections. This again explains, in my view, the 1937 statement of the *groupe du Lundi* and the attack on regionalism. Regionalism, according to Hellens's own statement 'empêche de voir et de représenter la vie humaine en largeur et en profondeur'.

5

As a poet, essayist, short story writer and novelist Charles PLISNIER (1896–1952) has lived and written both prodigiously and prolifically. He can be summed up as a kind of unbelieving believer, in many ways representative of his age, whose whole life has been a perpetual quest for that calm and quietude of mind and spirit that eluded him until the end. He was born in the industrial province of Hainaut, at Ghlin-lez-Mons, the son of a militant Socialist father and of a Catholic mother. The mother's piety was matched by the father's professed atheism (though in

E

point of fact he died a convert to Protestantism). How else could
a young, highly intelligent and sensitive man react to the inevitable family tensions a marriage of such minds produced than
by himself pursuing a philosophy of extremes? A student at the
University of Brussels, the young Charles quickly identified
himself with Socialism and then with the Communist Party. He
became a barrister at the Court of Appeal of Brussels, embraced
the Trotsky cause wholeheartedly in 1928, and then, dis-
illusioned in much the same honest way as Gide, he severed all
connexions with Communism and devoted himself entirely to
literature. The award of the *Prix Goncourt* in 1937 led him to
settle permanently in Paris, and from then onwards he issued a
remarkable series of novels and further collections of verse that
betrayed his tormented interest in man's need for salvation from
his own incompetence and error. Obscurely he felt that all his life
he had been gradually moving towards the truth. 'Il n'y a pas
d'errance dans ma vie,' he wrote in 1946, thus coining a new and
expressive word. And Roger Bodart was later to write of him:
'Errance ou non, peu importe. Ce qui est certain c'est qu'il est
allé à Dieu en boîtant; quand il ne pouvait y aller par le clair, il
y allait par l'obscur.'

His break with the Communist Party was marked by an essay,
Mesure de notre Temps (1932). A collection of short stories, *Figures
Détruites*, followed in 1935. Meantime Plisnier had been meditat-
ing on the theme of a long novel which would show how that
massive bourgeois structure, the family, had outlived all its use-
fulness and in its present state of decay was feverishly attempting
to ward off the inevitable. *Mariages* appeared in 1936 and caused
a stir both because of the extraordinarily evocative and accurate
picture it gave of narrow, provincial bourgeois life and of the
melodramatic *dénouement* that followed as remorselessly as in a
Greek tragedy from the shape and pattern of circumstances.
Plisnier was anticipating and in a sense preparing the way for
Philippe Hériat's *Les Enfants Gâtés* (1939) and *La Famille
Boussardel* (1947). More important still, he re-oriented Belgian
writers in the direction of the psychological novel and with
penetrating and cruel insight laid bare all the weaknesses and
hypocrisies on both the social and the religious planes of the
bourgeoisie he pilloried. In this first novel of bourgeois life

Plisnier introduces what is to become the recurrent theme of a kind of triple plot involving the ritualistic nature of bourgeois existence, the importance of maternal love, and the necessity for rebellious action. *Mariages* tells at some length how 'his' family is determined to defend its riches and privileges by all means, not excluding crime. And his heroine, Fabienne Fraigneux, does not hesitate (cannot hesitate) to take the only possible measure left to her to prevent the collapse of a booming industrial concern: she poisons her own husband. In this way, adds Plisnier, 'la société était tout de même protégée du désordre'.

Together with *Mariages*, *Faux-Passeports* (1937) is probably Plisnier's best-known work, and the work that secured him the *Prix Goncourt*. The book is composed of a series of five separate memoirs of supposed Communist agitators who are all expelled from the Party for Trotsky deviationism. All these agitators have one thing in common: truth, in their eyes, has one facet only and not several; nor can the truth change from one moment to another; they are intelligent people of implacable, inflexible will who can never compromise and must follow the hard road they have chosen in their own way. In a sense they all symbolize the striving to attain the true Communist ideal of Plisnier (or of Christ). The title of the book is also heavily charged with symbolism, and this has to be remembered in connexion with each story before it can be fully understood. False passports are not only the false papers used by spies and terrorists to cross the borders from one country to another. They are the public face of each agitator as he goes, misunderstood, to his own crucifixion. In one story, *Corvelise*, Corvelise the supposed coward dies a hero, and so achieves by his sacrifice another face and another identity. In yet another story (*Iégor*) the incorruptible hero accepts to be called a traitor, proclaims his own treachery, and so crosses the borders of death with his own false passport. In outward appearance he is a broken and destroyed figure. In the secret places of the heart he is the perfect hero.

Between 1939 and 1942 Plisnier brought out his five-volume *roman-fleuve* to which he gave another significant title, *Meurtres*. In this novel he returns to his principal theme, that of criticizing the attitudes of bourgeois industrialists and of tracing the corrupting and corroding influence of great wealth locked up in family combines. The hero, Noël Annequin, is depicted as in perpetual opposition to the social conformism of his family and as struggling, along with his niece Martine, to free himself from the fetters his family background imposes on him. The president of the Annequin industrial concern, the doctor and the priest are all in league to maintain the *status quo*. And in consequence Noël and Martine, uncompromising and single-minded in their pursuit of the truth, must encounter much suffering and become even the cause of shedding blood. Significantly they pass through a communistic and anarchistic phase and finally are permitted to reach towards the 'faith' that has so long eluded them. It is equally significant to note that simultaneously with issuing the novel Plisnier was also composing one of his best and most mature poetry sequences entitled *Ave Genetrix* and thereby acknowledging his present involvement with his mother's earlier single-minded Catholic piety. In one of the most beautiful and moving poems he writes:

> Maman, vous avez cru. Une image d'azur
> ornait votre missel et vous laissiez vos tristes
> mains, comme des oiseaux frémir aux pieds du Christ
> et vos pleurs se mêlaient au sang de Ses blessures.

> Alors, je souriais. Quel vin que le savoir!
> Je vous criais mon ciel, ma terre et mes genèses,
> et mes fureurs, et mon Éden; et la mère Eve
> était une guenon qu'un singe faisait boire. . . .

> Mais vous disiez: 'Mon fils, ton cœur ne s'est pas tu.
> Si Dieu n'existe point, pourquoi l'insultes-tu?

> Tu l'aimes. Il te voit, mal transporté de haine.
> Tu l'aimes. Il le sait. Il t'appelle. Il t'attend.
> Tu l'aimes. Tu viendras, sur l'épine et le temps,
> étendre sous son Corps, ton corps et ton poème.

> Tu viendras par les jours. Tu viendras seul et nu.
> Tu viendras, sanglotant.'
> > > > > > > > Mère, je suis venu.

In the few years remaining to him Plisnier wrote *La Matriochka* (1944), a three-volume novel, *Mères* (1946–1949), *Beauté des Laides* (1951). At the time of his death he was working on *L'Affaire Palmenaire*, a relatively short story centred on the plight of a heroine who has a guilt complex in that she feels herself directly responsible for the successive deaths of her father and her aunt. Few novelists have spoken of the mother-figure with such warmth and such devotion as has Plisnier in these later works. The direction in which his mind was now moving is clear: before the mother-figure, Genetrix, there can be no more lies; only the sad smile of the mother, always hurt, always understanding, before whom the clan must eventually incline itself and be silent.

The importance of Plisnier as a novelist lies not in his style (which is undistinguished), nor in his choice of subject matter, nor even in the fact that he made a deep and thorough psychological study of the present decay of the greatest of social institutions, the family, and so could bear comparison with Balzac. He is important because he could tell a convincing story that conveyed the tragic duality of purpose that is common to all men and that constitutes the central drama of their lives. He could do this because he sensed so acutely and suffered so acutely from his own duality. He is the true iconoclast, the true anarchist. His sentiments are always mixed. He feels a tremendous admiration for the solid structure of bourgeois respectability which demands so much heroism and so much self-sacrifice to maintain, and yet he is compelled to destroy what he so admires because of the dishonourable means employed to bolster up the honourable and the worthy. With one hand he caresses the age-old stones of the edifice and with the other he lays the dynamite charge that will blow it sky-high. Amid all the confusion thereby caused, one mediating influence appears – the mother (Genetrix) who enlightens all souls with her patient love and her understanding. The symbolism is obvious and need not be elaborated:

> Dieu me verra venir dans mes lignes amères.
> Il fera s'écarter ses anges trop penchés
> sur ce triste transfuge en état de péché.
> Je lui dirai: 'Seigneur, je viens chercher ma mère.'

CHAPTER EIGHT

Modern Poetry

I

WITH THE death of Karel van de Woestijne in 1929
Flemish poetry lost its chief spokesman. For thirty
years or more he had dominated the literary scene and
the only Flemish poet approaching his stature had proved to be
Willem Elsschot who, with a mere handful of verses, *Verzen van
Vroeger* ('Poems of Yester Year', 1934), established himself as a
model for the younger poets to admire. As the title of the
collected edition indicates, they are poems of his youth, but they
are of remarkable visionary power, in turn ironic and cynical
and yet deeply compassionate. The younger generation, who had
to come to terms with the topsy-turvy world situation that
followed World War I and who were desirous of building a new
world order in which the nightmare of war should be banished
for ever, could not but be impressed. By the same token a number
of them turned their backs on what they termed the anarchic
individualism of *Van Nu En Straks*, despised dilettantism in all its
forms, and preached a new kind of humanitarianism by which
the whole of the people should be socially, materially and
intellectually enriched. They asked that poetry should be a comforting but also an intensified form of communication. They
spurned the traditional forms of expression as such, claimed that
they were less concerned with beauty of form and expression
than with finding new formulas, and condemned roundly any
form of particularism or narrow Flemish parochialism. They
grouped themselves in particular around two new literary
reviews, *De Stroom* ('The River') and *Ruimte* ('Space') and
heralded as their chief spokesman Paul VAN OSTAYEN (1896–
1928), who in point of fact never collaborated with either of the

reviews, preferring to hold himself aloof and work out his own approach in his own way.

Paul van Ostayen was, in short, a quarter of a century ahead of his time and launched the new humanitarian and expressionist movement with the publication in 1916 of a first collection of poems, *Music Hall*, which brought a new lyrical note into Flemish verse and yet managed to escape the simplicities of Gezelle and the oppressiveness of van de Woestijne. The appeal of *Music Hall* lay primarily in the unanimist approach, in the freshness of the vision and its prophetic accuracy, and in its pathetic despair at the collapse of all moral values. The poet is one with Vildrac, Duhamel and Jules Romains, and his verse forms betray the influence of both Verlaine and Laforgue. A further collection of verse, *Het Sienjaal* ('The Signal', 1918), emphasized still more firmly this approach and more than justified the promise of the earlier work. There then followed a dada-ist period marked by the publication of *Bezette Stad* ('The Occupied City', 1921), full of the promptings of the subconscious, in which the poet conscientiously strives to be the mere interpreter of all the ideas that thus reach him:

> I will be stripped naked
> and begin all over again.

Finally the poet moves towards what he defines as pure poetry and gives us *Het eerste boek van Schmoll* ('The First Book of Schmoll', 1928), in which he tries to elaborate his theory that the sense of a poem is of little or no importance: what matters most is the choice of word, the rhythm, and the musical combination of sounds that compose the verse; the test of a poem is whether it has the power to move the reader, and if sound and rhythm alone can evoke the response desired that is more than sufficient. None the less, there must be discipline. The poet states clearly his premiss and then must hold both himself and his reader within the limits set by the original intention.

None of the other poets of the so-called *Ruimte* group has achieved the same distinction as van Ostayen, and the group itself was soon challenged in its attitude by another literary coterie, *'t Fonteintje* ('The Little Spring'), who, whilst acknowledging the necessity for new forms of expression and realizing the importance at least of van Ostayen, spurned all pathos and pretension, revered the traditions established by van Woestijne, and sought to remain faithful to the traditional themes of poetry. Theirs is a quiet, almost subdued approach, timid even, and they aim at being simple, direct and brief. The chief spokesmen for the group (along with Maurice Roelants) have been Raymond Herreman and Richard Minne.

Raymond HERREMAN (1896–   ) spent the first ten years of his life in Menin, the next ten years in Ghent, where he trained to be a primary school teacher, and finally came to Brussels to earn his living as a journalist. His first collection of poems (shared with Maurice Roelants) was published in 1914 and given the title *Eros*. By 1920 he had become the acknowledged poet and spokesman for *'t Fonteintje* and was formulating quite clearly the plan of campaign of his own group. Of himself he writes: '(My poetry) is a Mozart symphony in a minor key', and he claims for his followers that

> We have no banner
> Over our heads unfurled.
> With no drawn sword
> Do we tilt at windmills.

A dramatic fantasy that he published in 1924 won him the *Prix Brabant*, and then followed in 1931 his first major and mature collection of verse, highly symbolic yet simple in appeal and using traditional lyric forms, entitled *De Roos van Jericho* ('The Rose of Jericho'). In 1937 came *Het Helder Gelaat* ('The Clear Face'); in 1940, *Wie zijn dag niet mint zal ten onder gaan* ('He who loves not his times shall perish'); in 1942, *De Minaars* ('The Lovers'). He published a first anthology of his collected verses in 1944 and has since been a regular contributor, both as poet and literary critic, to various Flemish literary periodicals.

His voice carries always a quiet note of both persuasion and conviction. He takes his reader into his confidence and speaks directly to him of his own joys and sorrows and of his (the poet's) artistic and philosophical progression. His style is sober and of limpid purity. He never strives for effect, uses few adjectives, employs no striking imagery. Simply he hymns the wonder of

life and living and his own puzzled and amused perplexity amid
it all:

> How shall I sing the Song of Songs
> in my simple homespun style?

Richard MINNE (1891–   ) is by contrast more direct in attack
and more subtle, whilst remaining faithful to the sober tradition
of his group. None the less he is the most temperamental of them
all and accompanies unexpected turns of phrase and strikingly
fresh imagery with a biting irony and great sensitivity to the
moral problems of the day. His fame rests principally on one
collection of forty poems entitled *In den zoeten Inval* ('Sweet
Welcome', 1927), in which, beneath a mask of irony and
scepticism, he contrasts a love of life and living with the problem
of reconciling this with God's own existence. One Flemish critic
has called him 'a Vergilian sensitive' and there is much that is
apposite in this comparison. Minne polishes most carefully his
verse, strips it of any pretensions to grandiloquence, and
skilfully avoids the declamatory style of many of his contemporaries into which his choice of subject matter and his
intense indignation could so easily have led him. He has been
criticized for his somewhat skittish pirouettes and for his
occasional clowning. He never does this, however, without good
reason and he more than redeems himself from this charge by the
undoubted influence he has had on later poets in making them
avoid both the grandiloquent and the declamatory. He is the
poet of intense emotion concisely and consistently expressed,
taut and noble in his sentiments and yet readily and easily in
communion with all who will follow the lead he gives.

If the younger contemporary Flemish poets – and by these I
mean poets born either during World War I or shortly afterwards – have learned their lesson from Minne they have not
noticeably progressed in any given direction. Some try to follow
in the tradition of *'t Fonteintje*, others in that of *Ruimte*, and all
seem to hark back in some way or other to the individualistic
traditions established by *Van Nu En Straks*. Their individualism
has a romantic-realist approach, and they take as their themes
love, the family, the past history of Flanders and the queer

characters it has managed and still manages to produce, treating
the whole with common-place matter-of-factness. They re-
discover for themselves the Flemish landscape. They are on the
whole concrete in their approach and they seem to prefer
traditional classic verse forms to the blank verse of some of their
predecessors. The very youngest amongst them have (not sur-
prisingly) rediscovered Paul van Ostayen and are experimenting
along formalized and expressionistic lines, trying to discover a
new way of feeling.

Among these younger poets, Bert DECORTE (1915–   ) is undoubtedly the virtuoso. He writes in Latin as well as in Flemish.
He has translated Villon, Baudelaire and Rimbaud into
Flemish. He has issued a selection of translations of Japanese
geisha songs (*Yoshiwara*, 1942). His first book of verse (*Germinal*,
1937) aroused an immediate controversy in that some critics
hailed him as a new genius, palpitating with a richness of
imagination that he did not yet know fully how to control,
whilst others dismissed him as a pale imitator of Rimbaud and
van Ostayen. He confounded his critics by immediately producing another volume, *Orfeus gaat vorbei* ('The Passage of
Orpheus', 1940), in which he subtly presented heathen Greek
inspiration in a setting of Flemish symbolism. The same richness
of imagination, the same charming fantasy, the same subtle use
of rhythm were as much in evidence as in the earlier work, but he
had now learned to discipline himself and to show himself less
elementary in his verse forms and more conscious of the serious
purpose of the poet even when setting out merely to divert. This
book ended with a series of translations from the Greek, and he
now went on to show the measure of his self-discipline by producing a collection of three cycles of sonnets in which he carefully
retraces his past and in a mood of profound melancholy examines
the tension within him caused by feelings of lassitude and *ennui*
for ever warring with his ardent desire to be 'reborn' and to recapture that exhilarating paradise of the imagination of his early
youth (*Een stillere Dag* – 'A More Serene Day'). Latterly, he has
shown a distinct preference for the traditional French ballad
form, particularly that of Villon, and in *Refreinen* ('Refrains',
1943) his manner has again become more measured, more
austere, and increasingly captivating. His philosophy is closely

related to that of Villon, accepting life as it is, with all its contradictions, and finding in the mere fact of living an important objective. His last work, *Aards Gebedenboek* ('The Earthly Book of Prayers'), richly Bruegelian in conception, carries him still further along this path. Decorte is a poet only now reaching maturity and he deserves close study.

Herwig HENSEN (1917–   ) is in the direct line of descent from Van de Woestijne and none, since the foundation of the group *'t Fonteintje*, has written poetry so deeply introspective, following acutely yet objectively the development of his own abilities and analysing the conflicts of his own individual conscience. He is a teacher of mathematics and it sometimes seems that each of his poems is a kind of mathematical solution to the problem of living: he tries hard to find the correct equation.

His first collections of poetry were published in 1935 and 1936, when he was barely nineteen years of age. At the age of twenty-three he won the *Grand Prix Triennal de la Poésie* and eight years later was equally triumphant in the theatre. Most critics were astonished by his rapid development into a major poet and dramatist and felt, originally, that he was but a pale imitation of his acknowledged master, Van de Woestijne. Between 1938 and 1942, however, Hensen published six further volumes of verse that betrayed both an originality of outlook and a maturity of thought that went far beyond the tragic conception of existence of Van de Woestijne. In the beginning he had perhaps been a 'pale imitator'. Now, confident in his mastery of the techniques of poetry, he was equally confident in the importance of his own message and of his ability to convey its importance. The title of these various collections of verse have their own significance: *De Cirkel tot Narkissos* ('Narcissus Hemmed In', 1938); *Hamlet in den Spiegel* ('Hamlet through the Looking-Glass', 1939); *De dubbele Vaardigheid* ('Dual Disponibility', 1940); *Oefeningen naar binnen* ('Introspections', 1940); *Het voorbeeldig Bestand* ('An Exemplary Compromise', 1941); *Het onvoorwaardelijk Begin* ('An Unconditional Beginning', 1942).

It was in this latter year that Hensen turned his attention seriously to the theatre and many began to think that his inspiration as a poet had now waned. Once again he confounded his critics by bringing out *Lof der Gereedheid* '(In Praise of Disponibility', 1945). Here he continues the theme of 'An Unconditional Beginning' by affirming his belief in the necessity for accepting life as it is and by formulating his conception of the 'heroic life' to be lived. Fully to enjoy life, he claims, there must in this present age be deep personal introspection – a kind of *repliement sur soi* coupled with intense concentration. Further volumes, fortunately less cerebral and more easy of access, have been *Daidalos* ('Daedalus', 1948) and *Alles is Verband* ('We are all in Bonds', 1952).

He somewhat clarifies his earlier position by accepting life joyously and optimistically and by insisting on the importance of the desire to live. It is not a facile optimism but rather a mixture of hellenic stoicism and modern rationalism, tinged with melancholy at the thought of the chaotic nature of modern existence but insistent on the positive nature of the creative act. In Hensen's view the idea of creation is incompatible with pessimism which would negative all effort and declare all attempt at living 'absurd'. The desire to live, however, if it is to be fully successful must be carefully disciplined and the promptings of the heart must be guided by reason and intelligence. It is a stoic conception of life that Hensen opposes to the sentimental Christian attitude, and he is an atheist, a pure atheist in the sense that he does not even attempt to oppose the Christian ideal. He ignores it.

For all these reasons we find that favourite themes of Hensen are those of the mother, of the love of the child for the mother, of the husband for the wife, of the mother for her children, and of paternal pride in general. Nature as such plays a very secondary role in all his poetry. It has its important lessons to teach us, and that is all. Hensen has more recently published a cycle of poems entitled *Bezinning in eenzaamheid* ('Reflections in Solitude') dedicated to his wife and two children. It contains a poem that is worth translating in full in that it is a telling yet simple statement of his present position:

Do not the flowers bloom each year?
Do not the fruits of the flowers fall each year?
Life is none other than growing and hoping from the womb
And taking the quick, straight path to the tomb.

That is the rhythmic pattern of the life we know,
On which we build in calm, secure delight;
We know the regular sequences of ebb and flow
And how the darkness must give place to light;

And how in turn disease and death must follow
Remorselessly according to an ordered scheme;
And we are sad perhaps to find no other scheme,
Yet by acceptance so assuage our sorrow.

2

Modern Belgian poetry of French expression can be said to
have been rescued from the anti-artistic, anti-literary and anti-
poetical movement which called itself Dada by the determination
of one man, Franz Hellens. In 1922 he founded the literary
review *Le Disque Vert* and, along with his principal collaborators
Mélot du Dy and Odilon-Jean Périer, he proclaimed that the
rôle of the poet was to communicate as sincerely, as accurately
and as vividly as possible his interpretation of the universe. The
poet, as Périer himself put it, must seek for that purity of form and
expression which is not human but divine and therefore never
fully accessible. His quest is timeless and his concern not with
the passing political scene but with

> la marche lente
> Des choses qui grandissent, hors du temps. (HELLENS)

In other words, the true poet can never be *engagé*. The true poet is
a kind of priestess of his art and wedded to it until death:

> O tendresse de tes coups,
> Délices de ta morsure,
> Ton piétinement m'est doux,
>
> Délectable ta blessure.
> Ne t'arrête pas, mords,
> Agrafe à ma chair ta puissance,
> Cruauté de la jouissance
> Ne renonce que dans la mort! (HELLENS)

Mélot DU DY (1891–1956) did indeed devote the whole of his life to his poetry and worked hard to maintain in his own writings the high standards of excellence and elegance that were demanded of contributors to *Le Disque Vert*. Charming, debonair, gently ironical, he made a perfect host and a summons to lunch to his delightful country retreat at Rixensart more often than not prolonged itself into the late hours of the evening in repeated bouts of talking, reading aloud and producing variant translations into French from Keats – a poet to whom he became singularly attached towards the end of his life. His other great love was Ronsard, and as he stove to 'intellectualize' Keats (as he once put it to me) so he tried in some measure to be the Ronsard of his day and generation:

> Amour, dans le verger de l'automne, tu cueilles
> Un beau fruit rougissant sous la grâce des feuilles:
> Une guêpe s'y plaît qui te blesse le doigt.
> Cueilleur délicieux, mais cueilleur maladroit,
> Si ton désir enfin passe ta gourmandise,
> Donne à ton seul désir cette seule hantise
> Qui sauve du bonheur la douce déraison;
> Et dédaigne le bien d'une riche saison!
> Cueilleur ingénieux! mais viens, pour que tu ries,
> Viens ça, je toucherai tes mains fraîches, guéries
> Du mal que l'on se fait pour toucher à ces fruits.
> —Ha! Vénus et l'Amour dans les vergers détruits ...

If he is disenchanted with life and living (and this is often a pose to excuse his full acceptance of what life has to offer) he is full of no self-pity but manages realistically to become a mocking commentator, not only of the world's follies and foibles, but also of his own:

> D'autres répandaient des larmes
> Sur le genre un peu humain;
> Tu regardes cette lame
> Qui te brille dans la main ...

Or again:

N'aimez pas, disait Lucile,
Un poète. Ils ne font rien
Que s'aimer! De l'inutile
Soi-Même leur cœur est plein.

And finally:

Qu'emporterai-je, au temps de la grande Naissance,
Du fantôme léger qu'en ce monde je fus?
Le désir d'une erreur, le goût d'une présence,
Et le souvenir d'un refus.

His collected verse comprises *Mythologies* (1921), *Diableries* (1922), *Hommeries* (1924), *Amours* (1929), *A l'Amie Dormante* (1935), *Lucile* (1936), and *Jeu d'Ombres* (1937).

Odilon-Jean PÉRIER (1901–1928), without a doubt the major poet of this generation, is in direct line of descent from Charles Van Lerberghe yet manages to remain one of the most personal of modern poets. All his writing gives the impression of a burning yet strictly disciplined desire to 'refaire le monde à son image'; to bring us to share with him all the beauty he manages to distil from all the varied aspects of town as well as of country life, of friendship as well as of love; to urge us to do this whilst there is still time, for he will not dwell long among us:

Je ne chanterai pas très haut ni très longtemps

His high sense of dedication to his art permits of no self-indulgence and his verse must be stripped of all romantic absorption in the individual: a constant parade of personal emotions and personal preoccupations can lead to nothing but a dangerous kind of sentimentality that saps and corrodes the poet's genius and prostitutes his calling. There can be no self-deception. And, by the same token, the poet's audience must clearly know what to expect and also what is expected from it:

Amour, je ne viens pas dénouer tes cheveux.
Déserte, toute armée, inutile, étrangère,
Je vous laisse debout dans un peu de lumière
Et je garde ce corps pur et mystérieux.

Mais pardonnerez-vous ce merveilleux ouvrage?
Vous perdez un trésor à suivre mon conseil.
Comme une eau solitaire où descend le soleil
Renonce pour tant d'or aux plus beaux paysages,

Ainsi les mouvements, les ruses de la vie,
Ces faiblesses, ces jeux, cette douce agonie,
Vous n'en connaîtrez pas le redoutable prix.

Toute pure à jamais, mais toute prisonnière,
Vous resterez debout comme un peu de lumière,
Sans vivre, sans mourir, dans les vers que j'écris.

The rôle of the poet is to seek out the harmonies behind all
apparent disharmony and by the discipline he imposes on his
material make its message or appeal as significant as he can:

Bruxelles, arrosé comme une plante verte,
Bien nouveau, bien plaisant, se tait quand je le veux.
Ce n'est pas au hasard que je nomme ses dieux
Et ni distraitement que son grand corps murmure.

To do all this adequately he must be as limpid, as clear and as
direct in his approach as possible, and once again his reader
must know what he is about and make the necessary effort to
match the poet's own effort:

Je t'offre un verre d'eau glacée
N'y touche pas distraitement
Il est le prix d'une pensée
    Sans ornement

Tous les plaisirs de l'amitié
Combien cette eau me désaltère
Je t'en propose une moitié
    La plus légère

Regarde Je suis pur et vide
Comme le verre où tu as bu
Il ne fait pas d'être limpide
    Une vertu

Plus d'eau Mais la lumière sage
Donne à mon présent tout son prix
Tel, un poète où Dieu s'engage
Et reste pris

The collected poems of Périer were first published in 1937 and comprise *Le Combat de la Neige et du Poète* (1920), *La Vertu par le Chant* (1921), *Notre Mère la Ville* (1922), *Le Citadin* (1924), *Le Passage des Anges* (1926) and *Le Promeneur* (1927).

Eric de HAULLEVILLE (1900–1941) was equally preoccupied with the impossibility of ever approaching the high levels of perfection these poets set themselves—

Qu'as-tu fait de ce que je t'ai donné?
J'avais cru autrefois
Que de tes mains jaillirait
Un essaim d'oiseaux et de fleurs—

but he is much less reconciled than Périer to the essential loneliness of the poet. Périer hymns the drama of human solitude and escapes from his own feelings of isolation by crystallizing for us the warmth of his own reactions to town and city life:

Terrasse des cafés sous un lierre vermeil
D'où je vois s'agiter ma ville industrieuse,
Boulevard aussi beau par ta robe poudreuse
Qu'un fleuve déployé dans son vaste dessin,
Maisons de mes amis, la mienne, mon jardin,
Champs d'avoine et d'air pur qui faites la banlieue,
Nuages sur les toits et dans la pierre bleue,
Vous êtes le décor que je donne à ces vers.

Eric de Haulleville makes of his life a gesture of revolt and his early surrealist work betrays his impatience and his fervour as a poet. He cannot escape his destiny but he will make of it an adventure. And, after all, is not every poem an adventure in itself? Is not the dream but another aspect of reality and no less real than life itself?

A poem in his first published collection of verse (*Dénoûment*, 1923) has the significant title of 'Capitaine à son Bord'. He seeks to discover himself and to justify himself to himself by travel and by tasting life to the full, and yet realizes the fatuity of it all:

> Si moi j'étais toi que j'éviterais ma table!
> J'irais bâtir spacieuse ma vie
> j'irais sur les mers avec moi-même,
> et loin de moi m'égaler.
>
> Poète blessé,
> sur les lèvres le goût du sang,
> ouvre sur toi-même la croisée:
>
> Le jour baisse. Voici ta chambre se peupler,
> ton corps seul lumineux être la voile unique.
> Tu connais la folie à vouloir s'évader
> hors Dieu qui est en soi.

He travelled widely, dedicated an autobiographical poem, *Le Genre Epique* (1929), to the memory of Périer, was awarded the *Prix Albert Ier.* for his *Le Voyage aux îles Galapagos* in 1934, and published his last verses, *L'Anneau des Années*, the year he died. Gradually he became reconciled to the idea that

> Tous les sentiments que peuvent avoir les hommes
> Ont choisi mon cœur pour vider leur querelle.

He saw himself as 'seul sur la terre comme la noix tombée de l'arbre' and mocked at those who could not enter with him the *pays des légendes* and would not allow their children to do likewise, could they prevent it:

> La maman travaille
> Pour faire de ses petits
> Deux petits bourgeois,
> Ils vont éclore les petits bourgeons,
> Les sales petits bourgeois.

For Eric de Hauleville,

> La poésie commence à chaque instant
> Et chaque moment du paysage est un poème.

His desire for life and living is great and remembered place names pour from him in an evocative tumult of sound:

> Madère et l'Archipel, Malga, le Rhin, tout Bordeaux et la
> Bourgogne,
> Chypre, Alicante ou le Cap, la Champagne et ses arbres, Tokaï.

Finally, though he acknowledges the banality of human existence, he aspires to the rôle of the poet who can magically transform this:

> Je suis dans ce pays verdâtre et gris qu'un rayon de soleil
> Transfigure comme tes yeux matinaux ma journée
> Les peupliers aux cent et un miroirs où se regarde le vent
> Déclenchent une fragile mécanique d'orchestrion
> Au riche et monotone déroulement de légende . . .

and he reminds us that

> Il est de grands palais sous les eaux
> Où meurent d'ennui les sirènes maladives . . .

3

Henri MICHAUX (1899–) published some of his earliest work in *Le Disque Vert* and was in one sense trumpeted to fame by a small book André Gide devoted to his art in 1941 entitled *Découvrons Henri Michaux*. I say in one sense because it is doubtful if Gide ever really understood Michaux and also certain that Michaux had already made his impact as the outstanding living Belgian poet of his generation. All Gide did was to make him for a time fashionable. What Gide recognized was that Michaux hungered after life and expressed his hunger with the same burning sincerity as did Gide. What he did *not* grasp was that whereas he, Gide, hungered after life and had the earth as his kingdom, Michaux has never been able to satiate his most elementary appetites and in consequence hymns the emptiness of the world. Life for him is a sorry spectacle, a chaotic struggle, and escape from the futility of it all (which he roundly condemns) can only come through the invention of a newer and richer and imaginary world (full of illogicalities, contradictions and absurdities if judged by our sorry mundane standards) in which he and his reader who will journey with him are the irreplaceable kings:

> Malédiction sur la Terre, sur toute la civilisation, sur tous
> les êtres à la surface de toutes les planètes.
> A cause de ce vide!
> Ah! comme on est mal dans ma peau!

And so:

> Emportez-moi dans une caravelle,
> Dans une vieille et douce caravelle,
> Dans l'entrave, ou si l'on veut, dans l'écume,
> Et perdez-moi, au loin, au loin.
>
> Dans l'attelage d'un autre âge.
> Dans le velours trompeur de la neige.
> Dans l'haleine de quelques chiens réunis.
> Dans la troupe exténuée des feuilles mortes.
>
> Emportez-moi sans me briser, dans les baisers,
> Dans les poitrines qui se soulèvent et respirent,
> Sur les tapis des palmes et leur sourire,
> Dans les corridors des os longs, et des articulations.
>
> Emportez-moi, ou plutôt enfouissez-moi.

Born in Namur, and publishing his first collection of verse (*Le Rêve et la Jambe*) in 1921, he left the next year for a long and restless exploration of the two Americas. On his return he taught for a time in a college in the Ardennes, went to Paris and became the secretary of Supervielle, and has since led an essentially nervous and rootless existence, Paris still remaining his official base. *Qui je fus*, published in 1927, shows him experimenting with words and syntax in a fury of self-deprecation and of detestation of the world as he finds it, plunging into deliberate obscurity and ultra-modernism, and then producing his recipe for the voyage that must be made beyond the bounds of sanity if sanity and self-respect are to be preserved:

La vie est courte, mes petits agneaux.
Elle est encore beaucoup trop longue, mes petits agneaux . . .
Malheur à celui qui se décidera trop tard.
Malheur à celui qui voudra prévenir sa femme.
Malheur à celui qui ira aux provisions.
Il faudra être équipé à la minute, être rempli aussitôt de sang frais,
prendre sa besace sur la route et ne pas saigner des pieds.

His travels in South America resulted in the publication of *Ecuador* (1929) which left him still in a state of acute nausea and despair:

Rends-toi, mon cœur.
Nous avons assez lutté.
Et que ma vie s'arrête.
On n'a pas été des lâches,
On a fait ce qu'on a pu.

but which was to bring him some consolation in that it led him to a study of the Hindu religion which taught him how he could be united with the Eternal Self and so triumph over all material evil and corruption. From this point it is but a short step to discarding the material world, in which at the best one may only discover the appearances of truth, for a world of fantasy bred of the unconscious in which one may know one has reached to the truth because it is an 'invented' truth. *Mes Propriétés* (1930) illustrates this thesis, and in *Un Certain Plume* (1931) he invents a kind of Kafka-esque hero who, because our world does not and cannot exist for him, is disturbed by nothing and is therefore at peace:

Dans la brume tiède d'une haleine de jeune fille, j'ai pris place.
Je me suis retiré, je n'ai pas quitté ma place.
Ses bras ne pèsent rien. On les rencontre comme l'eau.
Ce qui est fané disparaît devant elle. Il ne reste que ses yeux,
Longues belles herbes, longues belles fleurs croissaient dans notre
      champ.
Obstacle si léger sur ma poitrine, comme tu t'appuies maintenant.
Tu t'appuies tellement, maintenant que tu n'es plus.

From here to madness is but one short step, and this he recognizes. Is not a lunatic a man who builds the world his own way? And do we not define a madman as one who explains the world away differently from the rest of us? If peace and understanding come only with madness (as so defined) then let the world go mad, for pity's sake:

Je vous construirai une ville avec des loques, moi!
Je vous construirai sans plan et sans ciment
Un édifice que vous ne détruirez pas,
Et qu'une espèce d'évidence écumante
Soutiendra et gonflera, qui viendra vous braire au nez,
Et au nez gelé de tous vos Parthénons, vos arts arabes, et de vos
    Mings . . .
Glas! Glas! Glas sur vous tous, néant sur les vivants!
Oui, je crois en Dieu! Certes, il n'en sait rien! . . .
Oh monde, monde étranglé, ventre froid!

Madmen in a garden of a lunatic asylum rebuilding the world. The one constructs a town out of a dice. Another out of a flea. A third out of an iceberg. And when their keepers try to tear the madmen away from their healthy pursuits, one madman changes the keepers into locomotives, another changes them into trees, and a third makes hills of them.

Icebergs, Icebergs, cathédrales sans religion de l'hiver éternel,
Combien hauts, combien purs sont tes bords enfantés par le
froid . . .

Icebergs, Icebergs, Solitaires sans besoin, des pays bouchés,
distants, et libres de vermine. Parents des îles, parents des
sources, comme je vous vois, comme vous m'êtes familiers . . .

The iceberg remains the symbol for his escape, the symbol of purity and detachment from the vileness of the world.

After the publication of *La Nuit Remue* (1934), from which the above extracts are taken, he turned with increasing invective to castigating the ills of the world and took his reader on an imaginary journey, *Le Voyage en Grande Garabagne* (1936) and *Au Pays de la Magie* (1942), torturing himself and his imagination to the maximum to show us, not *homo sapiens* but rather *homo delirans*. And then, in quieter and more sober tones, at the end of *Au Pays de la Magie*, he reduces Man to his proper size and gives his summing-up of the sorry situation:

Qui donc voulait sa perte?

L'homme à demi tourné vers moi était debout sur un talus. Il tomba.

Quoiqu'il ne fît guère que tomber du haut de sa taille, son corps arrivé à terre se trouva entièrement écrasé. Davantage: moulu, en bouillie, comme s'il avait été projeté du haut d'une grande falaise de quatre cents mètres, tandis qu'il avait seulement, dans sa chute, roulé d'un insignifiant petit talus.

Michaux himself seems to have recognized that the war years put an end to any possibility of his message being further heeded. The present nuclear age seems completely to have overwhelmed him and driven him still further beyond the bounds of real communication or affinity with his fellows. And, as though he recognized also that he had said as much as they could reasonably grasp, he issued in 1945 a definitive edition of extracts from all his previous writings with specific instructions to his publisher that these extracts alone should be allowed to survive. He called this book *L'Espace du Dedans*. With T. S. Eliot, Michaux might justly claim to be 'at the still point of the turning world', and from Eliot he might take his cue that

> There are those who would build the Temple,
> And those who prefer that the Temple should not be built.

To say that Robert GUIETTE (1895–   ) hymns the emptiness of the world like Michaux, but in a minor key, is not to belittle him. A native of Antwerp, he has been for many years Professor of French Literature at the University of Ghent. From his University Chair he seems to want to make of his poetry the kind of intellectual exercise Paul Valéry claimed it should always be. He has the academic calm and detachment that Michaux lacks, though it is allied to the same surrealist persuasions. Like

Michaux he began his career with contributions to *Le Disque Vert*, and he has since contented himself with issuing at rather lengthy and irregular intervals slim *plaquettes* of his amused comments on man's monstrous follies:

> Je flotte comme un bouchon
> sur l'histoire du monde
> —allez donc trouver
> un sens à tout cela!

At the same time, however, unlike Michaux, he finds himself always personally involved. It is as though he were writing to get to know himself better, to surprise himself, to deliver himself from the nightmares surrounding him by acknowledging an amused personal involvement. Sentimental himself, he tends to deride all show of sentimentality:

> Jean sans terre
> revient chercher
> la dernière pierre
> de son foyer
> Revient chercher
> la trace des larmes
> le lieu des rires
> Revient en vain

His is a quivering sense of solitude coupled with a stoical resolution to accept the 'emptiness' of the world:

> J'ai vu toute ma vie
> l'aube et le crépuscule
> sur le cœur de ma ville
>
> Pouvais-je alors savoir
> l'âme de son visage
>
> Mais voici sur la route
> son long regard lointain
> et son muet amour
>
> Ville qui fuit mes pas
> visage aimé de mon tourment
> l'enfant vieillit

> O ma ville grise
> corps aimé d'une morte
> mon cimetière
> moi-même

Yet, like Michaux, he acknowledges that

> La terre est en travail
> de sa folle agonie

and that

> Il n'y a plus de main que l'on puisse saisir
> plus de sol sous le pied ni de certitude
> Il n'y a plus de rive où l'on puisse aborder
> Il n'y a plus dans le vertige que l'Invisible
> plus menaçant que les ténèbres. . . .

> Tout le travail des hommes est perdu sans espoir.

Marcel THIRY (1897–) was still a pupil at the *Athénée* of Liège on the outbreak of World War I. At the age of twenty he found himself in Russia with a Belgian machine-gun corps. The Russian Revolution broke over him and he made his way back to his native Belgium via Moscow, Vladivostok, San Francisco, New York and Bordeaux – a complete world tour before fighting out the last stages of the war in Flanders. Where was he going? Why was he going there? Where was the world going? And where would it all end? He has been in a way obsessed with these thoughts ever since, but, unlike Michaux and Guiette, he finds himself necessarily involved with living and nostalgically regretting his inability to profit to the full from the adventures life lays before him. In this sense, life rejects *him* when *he* would more easily grasp it:

> Toi qui pâlis au nom de Vancouver
> Tu n'as pourtant fait qu'un banal voyage;
> Tu n'as pas vu les grands perroquets verts,
> Les fleuves indigo ni les sauvages.

He writes with lucidity and classical restraint, often in a mock serious vein, often reminiscent of Apollinaire, often happily wedding the traditional forms of poetry with the newer surrealist techniques:

> La mer s'en va comme ma jeunesse,
> Découvrant l'aridité des sables;
> O puissant reflux inarrêtable,
> La mer s'en va comme ma jeunesse.
>
> Mes lourds sourcils comme des tortues
> Vont fouissant leurs trous dans le sable;
> Fouisseurs aux lenteurs implacables,
> Mes lourds sourcils comme des tortues.
>
> O pour déterrer quelle détresse,
> Pour enterrer quelle autre jeunesse,
> Mes lourds sourcils comme des tortues
> Font-ils des trous comme des tortures?

He identifies himself with the tempo of modern life, and takes the motor car and its speedometer as symbols to illustrate his mocking yet sympathetic commentary. Thus:

> Quarante milles à ton compteur,
> Encor combien pour le bonheur,
> Cent cinquante pour Lunéville
> Et pour la lune trois cent mille;
> De Charleroi d'où je suis né
> A Charleville pour dîner,
> Les rois, les villes, les années,
> A-t-on passé l'Epiphanie.

Or:

> Je prends ma poésie à vos courbes, voitures,
> Je la capte, fuyante à vos flancs comme une onde
> Ou comme l'air dont vos profils prestes éludent
> L'emprise par une esquive de vive aronde.
>
> Je sais par vous que c'est de la courbe des gorges,
> De la fuite des reins, de l'esquive du col
> Que les corps, voyageurs par le ciel noir des âges,
> S'aident contre le grand vent debout de la mort.

The invasion of Belgium and the fall of France in 1940 drove Thiry into hiding and clandestine activities against the occupying forces. From these war years came some of his most mature and serious verse – notably *Prose dans Paris Sombré* (1941), Paris submerged in a sea of shame, a Paris in which

> C'est le creux, c'est le manque d'hommes, c'est le vide
> De pain, c'est l'absence des alcools aux terrasses
> Et dans le cœur le trou des soldats prisonniers

but also a Paris in which the hidden Métro, with its 'maternelles entrailles', remains a symbol of mounting hate which will soon vomit forth

> la haute flamme expiatoire
> D'un volcan de vitesse aveugle et de victoire

He also learned the important lesson that the modern materialistic age must reject the man who seeks to find in it only happiness. Acceptance of the age in which one lives brings not happiness but only a certain peace of mind and a kind of ever-questioning tranquillity of purpose and recollection:

> Un Souvenir géant sort des mers de la haine.
> Qui es-tu? Ton visage raconte une plaine
> Où nous aurions vécu l'enfance et le bonheur.
> Qui es-tu, naufragé vert d'algues, voyageur
> Qui meus pensivement comme une longue peine,
> A travers l'entrave des lourdes eaux salées,
> Tes grandes jambes qui refoulent les années?

Marcel Thiry has been a member of the *Académie Royale de langue et de littérature françaises* since 1939. He was awarded the *Prix Verhaeren* for his verse in 1926, the *Prix Beernaert* in 1929, the *Prix Triennal de la Poésie* in 1935, and the *Prix Albert Mockel* in 1958. The two most recent and representative collections of his verse are *Ages* (1950) and *Poésie 1924–1957* (1957). It is in the former collection (*Ages*) that he brilliantly sums up his mature reflections on twentieth-century Man:

L'homme est encor le poème innommé
Qui gravite à travers la nuit d'avant l'idée.
C'est la nue au tourment d'être consolidée
En soleil par son long tourbillon consommé.

L'homme est encor le verbe aveugle et qui s'ignore,
Plancton vague à travers la mer éternité,
Passif dans les typhons d'un éther agité
Où le sens du poème innommé s'élabore.

Comme, au long des virages du ciel, un essaim
Nébuleux, voyageur épars et sans dessin,
Rêve à finir au continuum de la sphère,

Un songe de figure et de rassemblement
Circule dans l'espèce et tâche obscurément
A la totalité d'un avenir solaire.

Géo Norge (1898–) betrays none of the inhibitions of this
present group of writers, but accepts life as it is, uncritically
almost in order the better to become its faithful interpreter, and
is in consequence himself accepted. In some respects it is not too
fanciful to call him the La Fontaine of his age, though, of course,
he is no fabulist. To him life is fun, and being just Norge is fun.
He is a sanguine connoisseur of all the many things that make life
worth living: wine, women, friendship, man and his conquest of
nature, and nature and its hold over man. He loves and mocks
and ridicules in turn. He caresses and he shows his claws. He has
almost a Bruegelian conception of living and depicts a contemporary scene in a manner his master would have approved:

S'aimèrent dur sous la lune
—Fers, aciers, métaux—
Pas de roses, pas de prunes
En ce pays sans défaut.

S'aimèrent dur, belle houille
Avec tes grains dans la peau.
Pas de lis, pas de citrouille:
Fers, aciers, métaux.

C'était riche et c'etait beau,
Cette lune sur l'usine,
Le gamin et la gamine,
Les seins contre la poitrine.
—Fers, aciers, métaux.—

Tout allait bien. Dieu sommeille
Et la guerre est en repos.
Belle amour encor plus belle,
O saisons industrielles,
Parmi vos grands végétaux :
Charbons aux fortes prunelles,
Fers, aciers, métaux,
            Poutrelles.

He knows exactly what he is trying to do. He gives us

            Une chanson bonne à mâcher
            Dure à la dent et douce au cœur.
            Ma sœur, il ne faut pas te fâcher,
                  Ma sœur.

            Une chanson bonne à mâcher
            Quand il fait noir, quand il fait peur,
            Comme à la lèvre du vacher,
                  La fleur.

            Une chanson bonne à mâcher
            Qui aurait le goût du bonheur,
            Mon enfance et de tes ruchers
                  L'odeur.

Of the many *plaquettes* of verse he has issued over the years, some printed privately, the most representative of his genius may be said to be: *Les Râpes* (1949), *Famines* (1950), *Les Oignons* (1953).

Robert VIVIER (1894–   ) is as much in love with life as Norge, but his is a nostalgic approach, tinged with tenderness and melancholy even, that veils his verse in soft pastel shades and gives it almost always a curious personal twist. He seeks the contact of ordinary men, the comfort of familiar scenes and places in order to escape

Toujours la familière peine
Qui me rappelle dans ma nuit

and to pierce, if possible, the miracle of human existence: why
ordinary men and women behave as they do; why they do
nothing to attempt to escape their destiny but on the contrary
both submit to it and savour it:

O nous que poussent vers la mort
Les rues des plus tièdes soirs,
Nous dont l'actif oubli dévore,
Comme un fruit tendre, la mémoire;

Nous dont l'âme use à son délire
Les vains courages de la chair,
Nous qui sentons les dents vieillir
Dans notre bouche solitaire,

Nous dont les lèvres et les joues,
Quand nul orgueil les surveille,
Désirent la terre et avouent
L'envie étrange du sommeil,

Iles que le mystère ronge,
Coeurs sans abri, tocsin qui sonne,
Nous,—ce mot rôde comme un songe,—
O nous qui mourrons,—*nous qui sommes* . . .

He had not yet completed his studies at the University of Liège
when World War I overwhelmed him. He fled to Holland, from
there to England, and then joined the Belgian army as a private
soldier. He later taught for a number of years in the *athénées* of
Hasselt and Bruxelles, and he is now Professor of French
Literature in Liège. These tragic war years undoubtedly left
their scar – 'nous avons tristement fait cette guerre', he says –
and brought him to realize that

le printemps de l'homme
Est lourd à naître.
Car l'homme doit trier ses routes,
Et plus d'un sort est caché dans son cœur.

Such is the theme of his novels, and in particular of *Mesures pour rien* (1947), and therein lies his inspiration for a most perceptive collection of critical essays, *Et la Poésie fut Langage*, first published in 1954. Poetry, he says, should be a kind of 'knot of humanity', a focal point, geometrically, where many people meet. And so, in a poem taken from his latest collection of verse, *Le Sang et le Murmure* (1954), he can say:

> Tout ce qui bouge sur la terre
> Et sur la ligne du sommeil,
> Les éclats les frissons et les songes,
> Pressés de vivre dans un être
> Formaient et déformaient mon corps . . .
> Les prés m'ont prêté leurs cils d'herbes.
> Sous mes chapeaux d'oiseaux siffleurs
> J'ai senti naître à chaque pas
> Un nouveau visage.
>
> Et peut-être un passant m'a-t-il,
> D'un regard ignorant, fait homme.

4

Two charming poets who, because of their freshness and directness of approach merit a section to themselves, would both eagerly subscribe to Vivier's idea that poetry must be where people meet. They are Marie Gevers and Maurice Carême. They are both concerned with the sheer magic of being alive, and equally concerned with sharing the magic and so strengthening its bonds amongst as wide a circle of readers as possible. For Marie Gevers, of whom I have already spoken as a novelist, any trivial incident of everyday life can become a subject for poetry: the fall of a leaf, the flight of a solitary bird, a child totally absorbed in play. She takes what we would so often dismiss as commonplace, shows us how wrong we are, invests it with a lilt and rhythm and makes it dance with gladness before our eyes:

> Juillet-aux-longs-soirs, la toupie,
> Chaque fois que nous la lançons,
> Nous lui donnons un temps de vie.

Le crépuscule tourne autour de l'horizon.

Elle frémit dans la poussière,
Mon chien l'examine et la craint,
Et si je la prends dans ma main,
Elle me mord de sa colère.

Et haut le bras, et corde au bout!
Si nous concourons au plus fort,
Je fendrai la tienne d'un coup.

Autour de l'horizon le crépuscule est d'or.

Elle vrombit, elle tressaille,
Heurte du flanc, saute, défaille,
Tourne encor deux fois et s'endort.

Autour de l'horizon, le crépuscule est mort.

Maurice Carême (1899–) completed his studies at the Teachers' Training College at Tirlemont and then went and taught in a primary school at Anderlecht (a suburb of Brussels) for twenty-five years. All this time he had been publishing novels, short stories, essays and verse, mainly for children, and towards the end of the last war (1943) he decided the time had come to devote his life entirely to what had become his abiding passion: writing for the people. Or, as he himself put it, whilst a Mallarmé, a Rimbaud, a Valéry are necessary for an intellectual élite, his kind of poetry is equally necessary to the child nature and the simple, unaffected emotions that are part of all of us and seek expression. 'Le poème n'est pas une expérience de laboratoire,' he says, 'ou un travail de marquetterie; son but existe avant tout à émouvoir, à exalter.'

His philosophy of life is simple and straightforward:

Il faut plus d'une pomme
Pour emplir un panier.
Il faut plus d'un pommier
Pour que chante un verger.

Mais il ne faut qu'un homme
Pour qu'un peu de bonté
Luise comme une pomme
Que l'on va partager.

In *Mère* (1935), *Femme* (1946), *La Maison Blanche* (1949), *La Voix du Silence* (1951) he writes movingly of family life and of his own parentage. His charm lies in his unaffected directness of approach:

Entrez chez moi, mon père, entrez,
Et que mon accueil vous soit doux
Comme l'était votre bonté
Lorsque enfant, je vivais chez vous
A Wavre, au milieu du Brabant
Où le vent, hiver comme été,
Chante dans les hauts peupliers.

and at his best he has in some measure merited the title of 'the Villon of his day' that Tristan Klingsor once bestowed on him:

Depuis le jour où tu es morte,
Nous ne nous sommes plus quittés.
Qui se doute que je te porte,
Mère, comme tu m'as porté?

Tu rajeunis de chaque instant
Que je vieillis pour te rejoindre;
Si je fus ton premier tourment,
Tu sera ma dernière plainte.

Déjà c'est ton pâle sourire
Qui transparaît sous mon visage,
Et lorsque je saurai souffrir
Longtemps, comme toi, sans rien dire,

C'est que nous aurons le même âge.

In his verses written especially for children he captures again and again the unassailable logic of the child mind, that logic we could always have held on to had we remained innocent, and a

F

logic with its own moral purpose. Notice in addition the deftness
of approach, the beautiful economy that leaves as much as
possible to the imagination, and the highly dramatic form of
presentation in the following:

> Dis, maman,
> Pourquoi n'a-t-il pas de roulettes,
> L'éléphant
> Qui tire la charrette
> Avec un clown dedans?
>
> Dis, qu'il est maladroit,
> Avec ses gros pieds plats!
>
> Est-ce pour le rendre plus comique
> Que le monsieur du cirque
> N'a laissé de roulettes
> Qu'à la charrette?
>
> Ah! Saint-Nicholas
> Serait bien étonné
> S'il voyait cela!
>
> Car l'éléphant qu'il m'a donné
> En a.

The sincerity and the transparent honesty of Maurice Carême,
coupled with a genuine modesty as to the lasting value of what
he writes, proves irresistible. And in one of his latest volumes of
verse, *Heure de Grâce* (1957), he humbly and all the more movingly takes stock of himself:

> Je ne sais ni jouer de vieux airs populaires,
> Ni même retenir par cœur une prière.
> Mais ce qu'on peut chanter pour se sentir meilleur,
> Je l'ai chanté, Seigneur.
>
> Ma vie s'est répandue en accords à vos pieds.
> L'humble enfant que je fus est enfant demeuré,
> Et le peu qu'un enfant donne dans sa candeur,
> Je vous l'offre, Seigneur.

5

The work of what we may call the twentieth-century generation of poets is dominated by Roger BODART (1910–) whose
first volume of verse, *Les Mains Tendues*, was published in 1930
and who, for his second volume, *Office des Ténèbres* (1937), was
awarded the *Prix Verhaeren*. Though he trained for the bar he
soon found himself devoting his whole time to literature. In 1952
he was admitted a member of the *Académie Royale de Langue et de
Littérature françaises*, and for a number of years he has been
literary adviser to the Belgian Ministry of Education. He sings
simply yet clearly of the life he loves: of home, of the family, of
the countryside; of the natural pleasures of ordinary existence
which are the only real and permanent things life has to offer:

> Dieu m'a donné la terre et ma femme en partage:
> Je ne puis que chanter ce que Dieu m'a donné.

When elsewhere I attempted to describe Bodart as a 'pure'
poet he rejected this appellation and preferred to speak of his
predilection for 'la poésie pleine'. By this he meant, as he has
been at great care to explain in *La Tapisserie de Pénélope* (1948),
that

> la connaissance poétique est une connaissance totale, de
> l'intelligence et du cœur, du corps et de l'âme. On peut même
> dire que la connaissance n'est poétique que dans la mesure où
> elle est totale, où elle est connaissance de l'être tout entier. . . .
> La connaissance poétique . . . procède de toutes les facultés qui
> permettent à l'homme d'appréhender la vie.

He then goes on to talk of the 'aimantations mystérieuses' which
attract the reader to the 'pure' poet, or to the 'complete' poet, a
magnetic form of attraction which weaves its own spell and
captivates the reader both by the sheer beauty of the verse and of
the message the poet is trying to convey. And the secret of this
bewitching as far as Bodart is concerned? First of all, a perfect
sincerity of expression. He tries neither to shock nor to foist on us
a pretentious philosophy. Of all that he is impatient. He is a

lyrical poet and his song is a song of praise and appraisal of the pleasures and perplexities of everyday life which he invites the reader to share with him. His faith in God is firmly rooted, and his regrets, his nostalgia, even his elegiac verse, draw comfort and inspiration from this faith:

> Laissons les autres croire encor
> Au grand silence de la mort.
> Nous deux connaissons l'alchimie
> Qui nous rend sans cesse à la vie.

His verse is full of overtones because it is so well chiselled and so well disciplined. He has a rare mastery of his art and he spares himself no pains to catch and hold a fleeting mood, a fleeting moment of beauty. And this also, incidentally, comes out in his prose criticism, notably in *Dialogues Européens* (1950) and *Dialogues Africains* (1952).

Gabriel Marcel sees Roger Bodart as in the traditional line of men like Paul Valéry, Charles du Bos and Edmond Jaloux, men who 'dans un monde en perdition ont gardé ce que j'appellerais volontiers le sens des repères absolus'. Maybe. But Bodart is all warmth and feeling. He may have the distant and abstracted air of the poet:

> Ceux qui me voient comptant mes rêves et mes pas
> Passer chaque matin près d'eux, ne savent pas
> Qu'un peu d'air étranger flotte autour de moi-même.

but he is also extremely human and vulnerable:

> Regarde. Je suis nu, grave et doux,—je suis comme
> Le cerf blessé qui lèche un poitrail roux de sang.
> Peu importe son mal. Lorsque le soir descend,
> Sa ramure est la harpe où le vent tiède parle,
> Et il lève le front pour brouter les étoiles.

Of his father he writes:

> Il retrouve son âme
> Comme un parfum perdu.

Comme un bois qui prend flamme,
Il meurt.—C'était son dû.
Son corps meurt. Mais son âme
Est un parfum rendu.

And of himself:

Je parle avec la voix d'un enfant étonné.
J'ai passé sans crier ni trembler dans la guerre,
Laissant d'autres parler de l'horreur des combats.
Je dis et je dirai ce que j'ai dit naguère,
La même paix du cœur, toujours un peu plus bas.

Auguste MARIN (1911–1940) was both the friend and disciple of Périer and also the friend of Bodart who, in a moving elegy on his death on active service on the banks of the river Lys, reminds us that

Toi, tu ne voulais pas sur ces routes nous suivre,
Et tu leur préféras ce voyage au long cours,
Ce redoutable amour plus pur que nos amours.

In other words, the anguish of living that Bodart can never escape and Bodart's almost romantic desire for self-identification with his native countryside is something quite alien to Marin's understanding. At no point does his verse touch on the tragic or the emotional. He is at all times the detached observer, the crystallizer of beauty:

Le ciel est lumineux des printemps revenus
     en robe de dimanche
et le vent laisse fuir les parfums retenus
     au cœur des roses blanches.

Ecoute la prière ardente du ruisseau
     et les coqs du village . . .
Le silence a frémi d'un premier vol d'oiseau
     à travers le feuillage.

Voici que le matin va célébrer l'éveil
     à son temple de marbre

> et l'on entend déjà les rires du soleil
> dans les branches d'un arbre.

Marin's first collection of verse, *Statues de Neige* (1931), won him immediate acclaim, and *Le Front aux vitres* (1934) brought him the *Prix Verhaeren* at the incredibly early age of twenty-four. In 1939 he published an extremely perceptive critical essay on Périer – and then silence. Had he lived, there is some indication in his last poems, published in 1949 under the title of *Traces*, that he might have moved away in maturity from willed detachment to a richer sense of personal and therefore inescapable involvement with the world:

> Homme que le malheur épie,
> brûlant d'un méprisable feu,
> —lueurs, ténèbres de la vie—
> tu reçois et délaisses Dieu.
>
> Tu peux reconnaître les lentes
> visiteuses de ton exil.
> Leurs yeux, leurs mains tu les inventes
> comme une eau fine sur tes cils.
>
> Entends leurs pas dans ta mémoire
> où le bruit d'ossements futurs
> impose à tes raisons de croire
> cette faiblesse de l'Impur.

Edmond VANDERCAMMEN (1901–   ) in a sense combines in his own work the approaches of both Bodart and Marin and also relates Belgian poetry of French expression to the unanimist approach introduced into Flemish verse by Paul van Ostayen. Faithful to his peasant upbringing in his native Ohain, he has constantly sought and drawn his inspiration from the countryside and sought to identify himself with it:

> Il n'y a plus que cette neige et moi
> Sur notre terre aux blessures d'hiver.
> Les rumeurs de l'amour sont des sanglots
> Que j'étouffe des mains pour mieux m'entendre.
> Je parle à la blancheur du paysage.

And, of his own work and his own peculiar approach to writing
poetry, he has written:

> Dans la certitude que toute aventure exige une issue, seul
> l'amour m'est apparu comme le don suprême capable d'y
> mener. Amour des hommes, des choses, du mystère cosmique, de
> la divinité même soupçonnée. Et j'ai cultivé ce sentiment, y
> découvrant de plus en plus de nouvelles raisons de croire en la
> beauté d'être. Je pense que la contemplation de la Nature m'a
> fortement aidé à accomplir pareille démarche; du moins
> m'aura-t-elle permis parfois d'atteindre une réconfortante
> sérénité.

For Vandercammen the poet's true territory is where he first
grappled with the mystery of being alive and related this to what
he terms 'la pérennité des choses'. Love of nature can be manifest in the study of a mere blade of grass which, in its turn and
properly understood, can and should reveal something of the
mystery of the whole universe. He hymns nature not for itself
but for its perpetual revelation of the eternal themes of birth,
life and death. And for similar reasons he identifies himself as
closely as he can with it:

> Je suis la mer, le sang du ciel et de la terre,
> La poitrine du vent, le sein des nostalgies,
> La blessure vorace au flanc de vos rochers,
> Le murmure, le cri, l'ivresse, la folie.

so that the very act of loving becomes but one part of a greater
whole:

> Jeanne, l'automne a commencé dans tous nos arbres
> Et les soirs sont si longs qu'il faut trouver déjà
> La prière du sang qui réchauffe l'attente.
> Jeanne, femme insoumise, immortelle, sauvage,
> Béate dans l'absence où s'égarent tes seins,
> Monts intimes voués au repos du péché;
> Jeanne des beaux matins et des fleurs onduleuses,
> Jeanne des bois, Jeanne des cieux, Jeanne des sources,
> Douce ténèbre qui s'avance dans ma nuit.

His verse is carefully disciplined but he rightly rejects the appellation of neo-classical that has sometimes been attributed to him. He will take the verse form that best suits his purpose and mould it to his purpose whilst preserving as far as possible its inherent structure. He avoids in this way with uncanny skill the twin pitfalls of sheer intellectualism (to which Auguste Marin is prone) and sentimentality (that sometimes betrays Roger Bodart). He acknowledges in this respect his indebtedness to his prolonged study of and love for Spanish poets – in particular Lope de Vega and Lorca, of whose works he has made excellent translations. He has recently published (in translation) an anthology of modern Spanish verse and has been honoured with membership of the Rio de Janeiro Academy of Letters. He has for some time been a member of the *Académie Royale de Langue et de Littérature françaises*, and his thirty years of active life as a poet was in 1962 marked by the publication of a selection of his best works. 'C'est une belle vie en poésie,' writes Jean Cassou in his preface to this collected edition.

Of Théo LÉGER (1912–   ) I have little to say in that he has remained silent since the publication of *Ornement de la Vie Intérieure* (1938) and *Andromède Ebloui* (1942), two works which in their richness of melody, purity and restraint of style and nobleness of purpose promised much. One still watches with interest the progress of Charles BERTIN (1919–   ), Jean TORDEUR (1920–   ) and Jean MOGIN (1921–   ), all of whom, curiously enough, have latterly turned with success to the theatre. Bertin has also written two intriguing novels: *Journal d'un Crime* and *Le Bel Age*.

CHAPTER NINE

The Flemish Theatre

I

IT IS A most interesting phenomenon that a small country of the size of Belgium should display such tremendous vitality and interest in the theatre as it does and, despite all modern distractions, still retain its hard core of theatregoers even in the most remote provincial towns. It is equally interesting to note how many dramatic authors of Belgian origin have achieved international fame – Maeterlinck, Soumagne, Crommelynck, Closson, de Ghelderode, Teirlinck – showing the way to symbolism in the theatre in the 1890's, to expressionism in the 1920's, and heralding the modern problem play in its diverse forms in the present post-war decades. It is a phenomenon that can be understood only when set against the background of the Belgian people themselves. And the kind of play the Belgian writes, as well as the nature of its peculiar compelling force (be it farce or tragedy), can again only be understood against this background.

The Belgian people are energetic, cordial and businesslike. They are stolidly good-humoured, even in the face of repeated adversities. They are possessed of a dogged tenacity of purpose. They are individualists, and with this individualism goes a quick temper to defend their rights and liberties allied to a shrewd realism and an eventual readiness to compromise. They jealously guard their traditions and are rightly proud of their heritage. At all levels of society they love pomp and display, show and pageantry and make-belief, and they will seize any opportunity to relieve the drab tedium of ordinary existence with some form of merry-making. They are a curious mixture of mysticism and sensuality, of religious scrupulosity and an almost pagan zest for living. They have never been better depicted, with all their sensuousness and love of colour and realism, than during the great period of flowering of Flemish art and notably in such paintings of Bruegel as *Le Triomphe de la Mort* or *Danse des Paysans*; in Jordaens's *Le Satyre et le Paysan*; in Ensor's *Mangeuse d'Huîtres* or his notorious *Entrée du Christ à Bruxelles*.

Thus, the Belgian theatre is a theatre of the people – of all the people – and it is a serious theatre in that each author finds himself the bearer of a message he has an overwhelming urge to deliver. It matters little whether the play be a gay domestic farce (like the traditional *Le Mariage de Mademoiselle Beulemanns*), a froth of a comedy (like Sion's *La Matrone d'Ephèse*), a patriotic piece (like Closson's *Le Jeu des Quatre Fils Aymon*), a grim comic charade (like de Ghelderode's *Hop Signor!*), or a haunting reappraisal of the consequences of the Crucifixion as depicted in Soumagne's *Madame Marie*. There is an important message to be conveyed and the spectator is irrevocably driven to some serious self-questioning. In this sense the Belgian theatre is in direct line of descent from the old miracle and morality plays, and like them it despises neither knock-about farce, nor poetry, nor the supernatural to achieve its aim. Its kinship with the Middle Ages is immediately apparent in the astonishing mixture of idealism and crudeness, of poetry with earthiness; in its tendency to incarnate ideas and create symbols; in its (often) dark Bruegelian humour; in the outrageousness of many of its comic situations; in its mysticism and in its striving for the absolute; in its very real belief in the Devil and in the omnipresence of Death; in its very real concern for the solitude of modern man.

At no time since the Middle Ages has life been so precariously in the balance. At no time since then has man been so perplexedly divided between his craving for material satisfaction and his yearning for that which surpasses him. Belgium, still the melting-pot of Europe and still at the crossroads of European culture and disaster, feels this probably more acutely than most other European nations. It is from this, I am convinced, that stems the present importance of Belgian playwrights, be they Flemish or French-speaking.

2

The Flemish theatre was slow to achieve European recognition and distinction in comparison with its French counterpart if only for the reason that the Flemings have always been better performers and spectators than authors, and also because the Flemish temperament tends to hanker after mass entertainment and participation. The Fleming is much given to processions and open-air spectacles, and from this longing for pageantry and group involvement in mystical and religious experience has sprung a whole serious of modern mystery plays, often based on local legend and tradition, and acted out against a natural background of medieval ruins, castles and cathedrals before audiences of thousands and with casts running into hundreds. Thus, the play of the Holy Blood, performed before the belfry of Bruges, has a cast of 2,000 and a choir of 800. Between twenty and thirty similar plays are to be seen every summer season throughout Belgium. They all comprise speaking choirs, mass movement of actors, intricate and complicated lighting, music and carillons, and – because the natural setting for the play is allowed to dominate the whole – staging becomes much more important than the actual text. It is a natural, spontaneous theatre designed to nurse vast audiences towards an approved pitch of religious or national fervour.

The first stage play of any historical note to be written in Flemish was the verse drama of Alfred HEGENSCHEIDT (1866–   ), *Starkadd* (1898), which owes its popularity more to the insistence of the dynamic director of the Flemish National Theatre, Oskar De Gruyter, on having it in his repertory than to its intrinsic dramatic worth. It is a kind of Schiller pastiche on the Hamlet theme and draws its dramatic tension from the juxtaposition of the virtues and defects of those who create a state and those whose duty it is to maintain it, once created. Raphael VERHULST (1866–1941) attempted to break new ground with a highly symbolic verse play, *Jezus de Nazarener* (1904), in which, although Christ remains the central figure, the main concern is with the effect on the bystanders of seeing real greatness and nobility of purpose doomed by deliberate refusal to use unworthy means to save itself. The approach is near-rationalist, and the miraculous is deliberately toned down to give added pathos to the tragedy. The priest-poet Cyriel VERSCHAEVE (1874–1950) wrote both historical-nationalistic plays (*Jakob van Artevelde* and *Filip van Artevelde* – 1909) and also plays on biblical themes of which the most successful were *Judas* (1919) and *Maria Magdalena* (1930).

Cyriel BUYSSE (1859–1932) was the first to introduce an authentic Flemish note into the theatre by writing a dozen or so plays with the same set purpose as he had written his novels. For this reason the plays are written mostly in dialect and they have in consequence not had the wider public they deserve. They are not problem plays. They indulge in no high flights of poetry. They betray no trace of the supernatural. As with his novels, Buysse attempts to be quietly realistic and to depict exactly what he sees about him. His humour is at once both ferocious and tender, and it is his peculiar gift of being able to detach himself from his characters to scrutinize them with piercing yet sympathetic understanding that makes him most successful at writing comedies. His very first play, indeed, *De Plaatsvervangende Vrederechter* ('The Substitute Magistrate', 1895), is probably his best. Georges Feydeau himself could not have bettered the mathematical precision with which the comedy is shaped, and, as a caricature of the judiciary, it preceded the equally successful judicial comedies of Courteline by some several years. In other plays such as *Het Gezin van Paemel* ('The Paemel Family', 1903) Buysse is in more sombre mood and reverts more closely to themes of his novels, in this case to the struggles of a peasant farmer against the nobility of the countryside.

3

None the less, it needed World War I and the determination and vision of Dr Oskar De Gruyter for the Flemish theatre firmly to establish itself as a European rather than as a local theatre. Together with a group of like-minded Belgian soldiers De Gruyter founded the Flemish Front Line Theatre on the Yser itself in 1918, and, two years later, the Flemish National Theatre.

He was intelligent enough to grasp that, if his ambitions were to be realized, then actor, playwright and spectator must all be educated together. To this end he renewed contact with the medieval Flemish tradition by staging miracle plays, farces and moralities; he established an *avant-garde* theatre by staging great foreign plays – amongst which Cocteau's *Orphée* had its real première in Belgium and not in Paris; and he encouraged the Flemish playwright by producing the best of his contemporary work that he could find.

Inevitably the Flemish theatre became an *avant-garde* theatre if only because De Gruyter was encouraging all Flemings in this idea, and, just as the theatre of French expression had earlier championed symbolism in the theatre, so now the Flemish stage stood firmly by Gordon Craig and for expressionism. The 'natural' word was to be rehabilitated at the expense of lyrical expression. It is the 'natural' word only which conveys meaning. The play, because it is *of* the people, must find its subject in the people and be played by and for them, with emphasis at all times on the acting. The sentiments of the people must be interpreted to the people. Nor should it be forgotten that expressionism and surrealism in art were then much in vogue and that the period of the 'twenties brought the silent cinema screen to a peak of perfection. In meeting the challenge of the cinema the theatre had to study the best cinematographic techniques. The Flemish theatre was singularly fortunate in that at this very time Herman TEIRLINCK (1879–   ) interested himself in the stage and in his very first play superbly demonstrated how the film maker's licence and skill could be wedded to the newer expressionist ideals.

The play in question, *De Vertraagde Film* ('Slow Motion Picture' – a significant title) had its première on 8 March 1922, and was an immediate success. Borrowing the technique of the cinema, Teirlinck presented the suicide of two young lovers. As they jump into the river they relive for the benefit of the audience all the memories that pass through their minds at the moment of suicide. As death lays hold of them they clutch violently at life to the point of clawing one another in their efforts to escape. The police drag them from the water. They regain consciousness, reproach one another bitterly and then go their separate ways, cured for ever of their passion. It was a brilliant technique to be used later by Salacrou in his *L'Inconnue d'Arras* (1935).

In 1923–24 Teirlinck experimented with two open-air plays, *Het Torenspiel* and *A–Z Spel* ('The Tower Play' and 'The A–Z Play'), and then gave us the somewhat scurrilous *Ik Dien* ('I Serve') in which in a series of astonishing tableaux he retold the medieval Beatrice legend, the second act of which became a spectacle given by the Devil to the populace thronging a village fair. *De Man Zonder Lijf* ('The Bodiless Man', 1935) was a variation on the Everyman theme, a personification of the different tendencies of one person, presenting them as separate entities. Teirlinck's last important work for the stage (before resuming his career as a novelist), *De Ekster op de Galg* ('The Magpie on the Gallows', 1937), betrayed a more rigorous technique, a greater sense of simplicity and a deeper awareness of the dramatist's capacity for plumbing hidden depths of human behaviour. It is a drama of old age in which the hero too late realizes that with the help of a too perfect wife he has forgotten how to live. He furiously desires to regain time lost, and in so doing precipitates a series of disasters that originate in the exercise of a too rigid virtue.

Teirlinck's importance in the Flemish theatre stems from his determined break with realism, from his desire to express important general truths in a kind of stylized version of life, from his willingness (and ability) to experiment with cinematographic techniques, and from his insistence on the playwright's need to recognize that he is but one element (if perhaps the most important one) in a successful theatrical production. Staging, costumes, lighting, scenery, music – all have their important contributory parts to play. With *De Ekster op de Galg* Teirlinck abandoned his earlier predilection for tableaux and disciplined himself to a two-act play in a single stage setting – what is sometimes called today simultaneous staging. Thus, he showed a room with an adjoining garden, a stairway and landing, and at the top of the stairs a platform which housed the observatory of his scholar hero, Benedict. Teirlinck's weakness as a dramatist is due to his supreme gifts as a novelist. For the theatre, his style is too finely spun and he has difficulty in allowing his characters to speak with a natural voice and react naturally to the situations in which they find themselves. It is to his credit, however, that he recognized this and that when he felt he had made what genuine contribution he could to the new Flemish theatre he returned gracefully to his main preoccupation.

Gaston MARTENS (1883–   ), on the other hand, is a natural playwright with an excellent photographic memory for sights and sounds, but unable to present and develop any really convincing plot. His language is rich and filled with atmosphere and he is primarily a caricaturist creating drama out of hearsay folklore and popular incidents occurring in his native valley of the Lys. His best-known plays are *Het Dorp der Mirakelen* ('The Village of Miracles') and *Paradijsvogels* ('Birds of Paradise'). The latter was adapted for the French stage by André Obey and had a tremendous success in the immediate post-war period in Paris. A film was also made from it, *Les Gueux du Paradis*, and starred both Raimu and Fernandel.

Anton VAN DE VELDE (1895–   ) is a playwright who has managed successfully to be both expressionist and symbolist in his approach and who, in attempting to raise the level of the Flemish theatre above the mere anecdotal, has imported a strangely wild and fantastic imagination to build a kind of bridge between medieval sensitivity, the sixteenth-century lust for rebellion, and modern Flemish nationalism. He made his début in 1924 with a strangely symbolic play, *De Zonderlinge Gast* ('Strange Visitor'), a play which married (not very satisfactorily) the deepest pessimism with the supernatural and which gave no hint of Van de Velde's exceptional gifts for depicting the fantastic, the burlesque and the droll. The visitor, of course, is Death, and the young daughter of the family visited, having successfully resisted the advances of the local schoolmaster, is strangely drawn towards the visitor who carries her off. Van de Velde reached his peak of perfection in two plays, *Tijl I* and *Tijl II*, which, though not an adaptation of the Thyl Ulenspiegel legend, brought a passionate patriotism to the theatre and became useful propaganda weapons for the revived Flemish movement. The effervescence and extravagances of Van de Velde's *Tijl* are matched by witticisms and sallies, by tender humour and the grossest of pleasantries, and by the expression of the most delicate feelings in the best possible taste so that the whole boiling cauldron cannot fail to captivate. The survival value of the plays, however, is doubtful. They are more literary curiosities, indications of the ferment into which the Flemish theatre was now excitingly plunging itself, a promise of better things to come.

The satirist of this generation is Paul DE MONT (1895–1950), whose work is characterized by unusually flexible and meaningful dialogue, which, however, sometimes unduly slows down the action of his plays. A conventional start with *De Spelbreker* ('The Spoil-sport', 1920) was followed up by *Nuances*, written in 1922 and first produced during the season of 1926–1927. Here Paul de Mont, who had returned from World War I a permanent invalid, attacks false patriotism through the eyes of a prince who once left to wage a fresh and joyous war and who now, broken and dying, rediscovers a true sense of human values. *Het Geding Van Ons Heer* ('The Trial of Our Lord', 1925) and *Reinart de Vos* ('Reynard the Fox') are his two most successful plays, the latter being a highly personal interpretation of the classic story that is packed with satire and political allusions. *Het Geding Van Ons Heer* is unique in treatment. Ostensibly it tells the drama of the Passion, but throughout it is a subtle attack on judicial procedure and it tries to prove how the justice of men must always be an imposture. Paul de Mont emphasizes this by dressing only the main actors historically and by insisting that the crowd shall by startling contrast be in modern casual clothing. The play hinges solely on the trial, sentence and execution of Our Lord, but again subtly focuses attention on the assassin, who is scarcely mentioned in the Gospels. It was this treatment which first gave Michel de Ghelderode the idea for his own highly successful *Barabbas*.

The only other two dramatic authors worthy of note in this inter-war period of expressionism are Raymond BRULEZ (1895–   ) and Willem PUTMAN (1900–1956). Putman, an actor turned playwright, had (as might be expected) an instinctive theatrical sense and wrote a number of well-tailored problemless plays whose very titles betray their sound entertainment value: *Olga's Ordeal* (1920), *The Quiet House* (1921), *Mama's Child* (1922), *The Dead Rat* (1924), and *Looping the Loop* (1925). Oskar De Gruyter was beginning to scrape the bottom of the barrel, and the only real new flash to match Teirlinck came with the production in 1936 of Brulez's *De Schone Slaapster* ('The Sleeping Beauty'). A girl falls asleep in 1815 when the French are enemies of Belgium and the Germans her allies. She reawakens in 1914 and has to adjust herself to the changed situation.

Oskar De Gruyter had, however, achieved his objective. The inherent weaknesses of expressionism in the theatre had become obvious in the process, it is true. It was difficult to refute the acid charge of Vermeylen that the true artist was the electrician. It had to be admitted that the prestige of the producer often outshone that of the author and pushed him into the background. Nevertheless it had to be conceded that out of all this had grown a thriving National Flemish Theatre and that Flemings had been made theatre-conscious as never before. Furthermore, Flemish playwrights were achieving both recognition and respect well beyond the confines of either Belgium or Holland. The terrain was well prepared for a new generation of playwrights. And as World War II ended so was expressionism finally abandoned in favour of what has come to be termed the literary theatre.

4

The younger playwrights of this present post-war period are experimenting in a variety of ways, and amongst them Tone BRULIN (1926–) has given us an interesting dramatized study of Vincent Van Gogh. Hugo CLAUS (1929–) in *The Song of the Murderer* allows a highwayman to relate his chaotic emotional life in a series of flashbacks. Marcel COOLE (1913–) symbolizes the conflict between personality and state power in *Achnaton*, and in *This Difficult Life* tries to suggest some solution to the problems of the young in this difficult disruptive post-war period. Jozef VAN HOECK (1922–) in *Sauternes, 1925*, exploits the dramatic possibilities of a conscience-ridden family and in *Provisional Judgement* deals with the conscience of an atomic physicist. Piet STERCKX (1925–) grapples with the existentialist nature of modern life, and in such plays as *The Lost Plant*, *Sonata for Two Hinges*, and *Hooks and Needles* alternates nonsense with deep melancholy and through this alternation tries to find the meaning of life.

All these young and still maturing playwrights are over-shadowed, however, by Johan DAISNE (1912–) and Herwig HENSEN (1917–). Daisne brings the same kind of magic-realism, the relating of the life of reality and actuality to that of the dream state, from his novels to the stage. In all he has given us four very remarkable plays: *Charade for Advent* (1943), *Tristan's Sword* (1944), *Tine van Berken* (1945), and *Veva* (1946). The last three plays form a kind of trilogy to develop a theme dear to Daisne, namely that it is love and love alone that can attain the divine. The divine *is* love. All earthly love, however, is a chimera in the sense that it is but a reflection of values un-attainable on this earth. We must renounce it, therefore, in favour of platonic love if we are to attain to perfection in love in the hereafter, and he symbolizes all this by the sword that is placed between Tristan and Isolde.

Herwig Hensen is obviously the more popular of the two play-wrights if only because he is the more readily accessible and understood. His first published play was a kind of romantic Shakespearean drama, *Antonio* (1942), and this was followed in 1943 by *Don Juan*. Then, in 1946 came the publication and performance of three other plays, *Lady Godiva*, *Queen Christina* and *Polycrates*. Then three more – *Alcestis*, *Agamemnon* and *Tarquin* – and Hensen had found his way to maturity and the kind of message he wished to put over. He is at his best when he dresses up a classical theme to express his own personal philosophy, and this philosophy can be summed up simply as a philosophy of provocation, of pride, of rebellion in an attempt to keep the personality intact and alive. Of all the plays *Lady Godiva* perhaps illustrates best Hensen's method.

The programme note from Hensen at the time of production of *Godiva* by the Flemish National Theatre stressed that all he knew of the Godiva legend was that Lady Godiva had ridden naked through the streets of Coventry as a challenge in order to stop the people being unduly oppressed by taxation. More than that he did not wish to know. He now asked himself why Lady Godiva was impelled to make this sacrifice. How did her husband come to allow it to happen? How did Lady Godiva, and her husband, and the young Percy who worshipped Lady Godiva all react to the consequences of the terrible ride? The answers to all these questions constitute the play. Lady Godiva accepts the challenge put to her by her brutal husband less out of charity for her subjects than out of pride and a kind of Nietzschean predilection for the impossible or the revolting. On her return her coarse and brutal husband becomes sentimental. The young Percy who thought he had loved her finds his love disappear. And Lady Godiva, misunderstood by husband and lover, and the subject of coarse jokes amongst the people she has tried to help, becomes a prey to cynicism and despair.

With *Polycrates*, Hensen first tackled the problem of real happiness being linked to an acceptance of death, to coming to terms with death, and he developed this theme with brilliant success in *Alcestis*, prefacing the printed version of his play with a quotation from Bertrand Russell: 'All fear is bad and ought to be overcome, not by fairy tales but by courage and rational reflection'; and developing Seneca's dictum that he who has learned to die has ceased to be a slave. Again, Hensen twists the Alcestis legend brilliantly to suit his own purpose and manages to portray Hercules most convincingly as an impudent bluffer and impostor. He reduces the gods of antiquity to trivial human proportions, makes Hercules proclaim that 'man does not believe what he ought to believe but what he wants to believe', and so prepares the ground for his fierce onslaught on blind obscurantism, ignorance and prejudice which in *Agamemnon* he centres on the classical theme of Iphigenia's sacrifice. In *Tarquin* he develops the idea that even error is preferable to knowledge based on the supernatural, for such divination means enslavement and the loss of all personal liberty.

Thus Hensen's tremendous appeal to the modern playgoer depends primarily on the fact that he is *engagé* in the best sense of the word: to assert his freedom and individuality man must make his own choice and then stand by the consequences. His choice made, he must defend it passionately and with all the lucidity of purpose he can muster. Hensen is also a superb craftsman in the theatre. He is full of things he wants to say, and in the saying of them makes his plays move at a fast tempo. Not a moment is wasted, there are no tedious repetitions, the play is constructed with mathematical precision, and the language is the language of the poet – charged with meaning, full of nuances, concise and lyrical. Hensen's importance in the history of the development of the Flemish theatre is that he is the first playwright successfully to divorce it from expressionism, to disdain the experimental and the obsession with things Flemish, and to treat with classical restraint and intensity the universal themes of man living, man marvelling, man dying.

CHAPTER TEN

The Theatre of French Expression

I

IN DISCUSSING the work of Maurice Maeterlinck we have
already stated that symbolism in the theatre was born and
died with him. We have also hinted, however, that Maeterlinck's influence could be held to extend much further than has
been generally supposed. And, quite naturally, this is nowhere
better in evidence than in the later development of the theatre
of French expression within Belgium itself. The only outstanding
contemporaries of Maeterlinck in the Belgian (French) theatre
had been Van Lerberghe (whose plays we have already discussed) and Verhaeren. Verhaeren was responsible for a forceful
and solidly built play, *Le Cloître* (1900), in which the entire action
is laid in a monastery. The protagonist, a monk named Dom
Balthasar, is destined to become prior of his monastery, but
suddenly publicly accuses himself of a crime committed long
ago and for which he has already had absolution. This causes a
scandal and affords a pretext to his brother monks to deny him
the office of prior. Dom Balthasar falls into the sin of pride by
pursuing his humiliation to the bitter end. The play is written
partly in prose and partly in verse and achieves its dramatic
intensity neither through mysticism nor through morbidity, but
through the forceful clash of strong characters. In affinities it
probably lies closest to the neo-romanticism of Edmond Rostand.

Thus, whilst the Flemish theatre established itself during the
1920's on a basis of expressionism, its French counterpart tended
to by-pass or transcend this through the examples set by Maeterlinck and his contemporaries. Of this new generation of playwrights Fernand CROMMELYNCK (1885–) is easily the most
oustanding and was, in the period between the two wars,
coupled in reputation with Jean Giraudoux. His earliest efforts,

first produced in 1906, 1911 and 1913, owed much to Maeterlinck's influence, were pleasantly received, but made little
impact. Then came *Les Amants Puérils* (1918), a play of considerable poetic charm though somewhat lacking in dramatic shape,
but a play in which Crommelynck for the first time revealed his
extraordinary command of words, loosening the ties language
has with the rational and exploring to the full all the power of
suggestion that can lie behind an apparently simple straightforward statement. In *Les Amants Puérils* in particular he piles
image and evocation on top of each other so that we have a kind
of vision of what the characters are thinking and saying, and he
makes frequent use of the conjunction 'comme' the better to
release the flood of images:

> Mais je grimperai comme un gamin dans un pommier en fleurs.
> J'arracherai une branche souple, j'en fouetterai l'air en marchant
> et là-bas je te l'offrirai. Et je dirai: je suis son écharpe, ses bagues,
> ses sandales, son rire et les rêves de son long sommeil.

What is generally hailed as Crommelynck's masterpiece, *Le
Cocu Magnifique*, came two years later in 1920, and was first
produced in Paris by Lugné-Poë. Bruno and Stella are two
devoted young lovers, and so proud is Bruno of his wife's beauty
that he wants to see all his friends in open admiration. One day,
however, he thinks he notices a gleam of desire in his cousin
Petrus's eyes and he slaps him. The die is cast. Jealousy and doubt
now both hold Bruno remorselessly in their grip. He locks his
wife up to hide her from everyone. But that only intensifies his
doubts and uncertainty. So he must release her and deliberately
throw her into the arms of other men to provoke the catastrophe
he fears. This only worsens his plight, for having originally
doubted her fidelity he now begins to doubt her infidelity! The
climax of this growing and almost unbearable dramatic tension
is reached when poor Stella is driven beyond endurance to
escape his clutches by fleeing with a most ordinary and commonplace individual. Bruno treats it all as a huge joke and fails to
realize that he has lost her for ever.

Crommelynck labelled this play a farce but it is a farce of
savage intensity with a wealth of undercurrent of meaning.

Bruno is not so much the jealous husband as the incarnation of jealousy itself, yet, as in a comedy by Molière, he remains pathetically human. All the characters, indeed, display their fundamental humanity in what has become for them an inhuman situation beyond their contriving. Or, as Roger Bodart has pertinently put it, Crommelynck does not so much show us characters as beings carried away by the folly of being. Crommelynck's world is the world of tragic buffoonery. Behind the farce lies the tragedy, the sin of being, a Bruegelian brooding on man wasting the brief span of his life on idle worries and being compelled to wear the mask, wrought of his own futility, that destiny finally imposes on each one of us. Thus, Crommelynck lacks the telling simplicity of Molière, is more sensual than cerebral in his approach, and does not so much explain his characters as throw light on them as they twist and turn in a kind of mimed choreography by cascading about them his rich, warm, beautiful and poetic prose.

Tripes d'Or, first produced by Louis Jouvet in 1930, is Crommelynck's strongest and most sombre play in that it is a kind of modern *sottie* – a tremendous farce in which the miser, Hormidas, though he passionately declares his love for Azelle, neglects her because of the avarice that holds him in its grip. The genius of Crommelynck as a dramatist becomes most evident in this play in that, though Azelle never once appears on stage, we come to know her perfectly through the rapturous descriptions given of her by Hormidas and through his anguished state of mind in no longer wishing to possess her and yet still ardently worshipping her beauty. The climax of the play is reached when it is announced that she is arriving. She is at the door. She knocks to seek admittance. Hormidas, held prisoner by his hoard of gold, forbids her to enter. It is difficult to realize that one does not see her there, behind the door, trembling with apprehension, moist-eyed and growing fainter with despair. The knocking dies away. . . . If only we could rush onto the stage and open the door to her . . . The knocking ceases . . . She is gone, for ever . . . And Hormidas greedily swallows his gold and bursts in the process of delivering himself of it!

Two further noteworthy plays of Crommelynck are *Une Femme qu'a le Cœur trop Petit* and *Chaud et Froid*, both produced in

Paris in 1934. The former play has several affinities with Teirlinck's *Magpie on the Gallows* (1937), which it is said to have inspired. Crommelynck also treats of a man who, having married a too perfect wife, is in danger of forgetting how to live. But there all comparison ends. Crommelynck's play is a mad, poetic caper, a pirouetting play in which the influence of the too-perfect wife casts its spell on all, and not least on the wife herself, Balbine. A delicious pair of rustic simpletons become intelligently and saucily dishonest in the process. Sensuality holds sway because of Balbine's fierce condemnation of it. And in her very hatred of lying she drives others to lies and deceit and her husband to a clear assessment of her own failing:

> Elle ne peut mentir, elle est le mensonge debout . . . Elle est le mensonge innocent. Elle ignore la vérité des hommes et des jours. Ses vertus n'ont aucune racine dans l'amour.

Chaud et Froid, in comparison with the other major plays of Crommelynck, suffers from a lack of definition of the characters involved and belongs much more to the world of choreography and mime than to the real theatre. It turns on the simple theme of inconstancy. Léona, the heroine, is capable of loving all men except her lawfully wedded husband, Dom. Félie, on the other hand, can love only Dom. When the mysterious Dom dies (he never once appears) and directs in his will that a place shall be specially reserved by his side in the grave for his childhood sweetheart, Félie, the roles become suddenly reversed: Léona grows to full stature as the faithful widow and Félie succumbs to the advances of a former lover of Léona, this at the contrivance of Léona. The point is that the contrivance works and in working it Léona has to accept her self-imposed destiny. Dramatically the play is saved by the rich, warm and colourful prose style Crommelynck has evolved and which he manages in a most uncanny way so that we have to accept it as the only possible manner of speech of the various protagonists in his charade.

2

Michel de GHELDERODE (1898–1962) has obvious affinities with Crommelynck and like him owes much to the influence of Maeterlinck. He has the same Bruegelian conception of human nature as Crommelynck, the same obsession with man's essentially sinful state, the same uncanny way of presenting his characters so that every apparently superficial remark is often found to be charged with hidden meaning and grim portent. The main difference between de Ghelderode and Crommelynck is that Crommelynck remains all the time essentially human and carefully keeps us this side of the brink that leads to goodness knows what folly and madness. Ghelderode is a Fleming 'de cœur et d'âme' and nostalgically harks back again and again to the Flanders that was (in all its coarseness and brutality) and never again will be. It is a nightmare world he presents to us, spun from the imagination of a solitary who got his greatest inspiration from gazing down on the decaying splendour of twentieth-century Bruges and declaring it to be 'one of the most beautiful stage settings in the world, a scene ready made'.

Ghelderode, like Crommelynck, builds on the drama of sin, but whilst Crommelynck believes only in the power of evil, Ghelderode really believes in the existence of the Devil, not only as a very real person, but also as a projection into the lives and affairs of so many people, very much like the devils of the medieval miracle and morality plays. The realm of black magic, of incantation and voodoo, is again real to him and he ends by turning himself into a kind of priest-anchorite of the theatre, spinning his plays in solitary self-absorption and totally indifferent to any success that may come his way. It is for these reasons that, though he has given us more than fifty plays (the most representative now collected into a five-volume edition by Gallimard), he worked in complete obscurity for over twenty years and was content to do so, being only proud of the fact that a Flemish version of his religious play *Barabbas* was performed every Easter in Flanders as a popular anonymous work. Jean-Louis Barrault 'discovered' Ghelderode immediately after the last war. For the next few years he was a popular success on the Parisian stage and his fame gradually spread abroad. To all this he remained supremely indifferent and aloof and never once left his closely-shuttered house in Brussels to attend even the most important of first nights!

Ghelderode was a solitary and introspective child, endowed with a mother who claimed to have seen the Devil in person, and a father who spent his life obscurely as an archivist. The home was overflowing with ancient documents, and the father's only means of communicating to his son the affection he undoubtedly felt was to make macabre dog-Latin jokes to amuse him. From the so-called 'Ostend Interviews' with Ghelderode we learn that he too worked as an archivist before entering into active collaboration with the Flemish Popular Theatre after the production in 1927 of his play *Saint François d'Assise* – a play which both outraged and delighted audiences with its displays of pantomime miracles and angels swinging on trapezes! This association lasted for only three years, however, and Ghelderode then completely withdrew into the solitude he came increasingly to recognize as his native element.

A serious illness at the age of sixteen started him on his writing career and he admits quite freely the tremendous influence that Charles de Coster's *Thyl Ulenspiegel* had on him at the time. He loved puppet shows, old dusty theatres, old churches and funerals ('only the Church buries well'), and as he grew older and came to recognize the affinities he had with Kyd, Marlowe, Ben Jonson, Tourneur, Massinger and Ford, so he felt powerfully drawn towards painters like Pieter Bruegel, Hieronymus Bosch, Teniers, Jordaens and James Ensor. Bruegel's painting, 'The Parable of the Blind Men', led him to write *Les Aveugles* (1933), which was first produced in Paris in 1956. Another Bruegel painting inspired *La Pie sur le Gibet* (1935), and he claims that in *Masques Ostendais* (1935) all he had done is to bring to life, and to pantomime, one of Ensor's paintings. He was equally influenced by the Germans von Arnim and Hoffmann, by the gothic tales of Horace Walpole, Ann Radcliffe, 'Monk' Lewis, by the stories of Edgar Allan Poe – and, of course, by Hugo's *Notre Dame* and *L'Homme qui Rit*. He worked, so he said, by vision and divination alone. And he saw what he had written as being an extended comedy of both good and evil. Sincere Catholic that he is, he is neither anti-clerical nor pro-clerical. He neither condones nor condemns. He reveals man as he is, in his brutal and fallen state with all the trappings (and possibilities) of greatness about him. His originality stems from the fact that he sees everything, as did Bruegel, from the people's point of view, or (as he himself has put it) 'from beneath'.

Barabbas perfectly illustrates this technique. The success of *Saint François d'Assise* stimulated the Flemish Popular Theatre to commission a play from Ghelderode that could be performed (in Flemish) in Holy Week, 1928. The idea of a play on the Crucifixion had long been maturing in Ghelderode's mind – a play in which Barabbas should be presented not as a bandit but rather as a folk hero, and also one in which the audience would be forced to witness the crucifixion and the sufferings of Jesus both from the point of view of Barabbas and from the point of view of the simple, earthy slum-dwellers of Jerusalem. As we have already noted, this Flemish version that Ghelderode now offered up has since been regularly performed in Holy Week in Flanders. The original French version was first performed in Brussels in 1934, revived in 1954 there, first produced at the Théâtre de l'Œuvre in Paris in 1950 and revived again there in 1956, this time being performed by the *Théâtre National de Belgique* at the *Théâtre Sarah-Bernhardt*. Its success has been phenomenal, and if it is not to be considered his most mature play (in comparison with his best work it must be ranked dull and too rhetorical) it is certainly amongst the most important.

Christ has been imprisoned along with Barabbas and the two thieves, but so dark and foetid is this prison that neither Barabbas nor his accomplices nor the spectator are aware for some time that Christ is there. When the revelation is at last made, what a picture! This is no King of the Jews, and not even a man, but a broken mass of flesh and bone, befouled, spat upon, bloody and crowned with thorns. If He is still alive it is because He has not yet suffered enough. Even Barabbas is aghast. The tragic drama unfolds itself whilst strolling players and sideshow men (one of whom is named Barnum) prepare feverishly for the funfair to entertain the crowd on Mount Golgotha and coax the money out of their pockets once the main diversion of the day (Christ's death) is over. It is a bustling, Bruegelian scene, with all its coarseness and lasciviousness:

> Entrez! Entrez! Venez voir les hommes du jour représentés par un illusionniste incomparable! Venez voir les célébrités, assassins et hommes politiques! Le vrai portrait de Barabbas! Entrez, on paie en sortant! La parade va commencer! Et après ce que nous allons vous montrer, vous jugerez de ce qu'on peut voir à l'intérieur! Approchez!

The agony of the actual crucifixion is told by an observer perched on a ruined flight of steps set in the funfair area, and is commented upon by Mary Magdalene and also the apostles who have deserted Christ and sought anonymity among the rabble in the funfair. The noise this milling crowd makes rises to a crescendo as Christ expires. An awful drawn-out silence. And then Barabbas comes into his own as the one person unafraid to champion Christ and thereby destined to be stabbed to death from behind, furtively, by a clown to whom he has already administered a thrashing for daring to mock Christ. As he expires he turns towards the Cross and the curtain comes down on his dying words:

> Et je saigne. Hé! Jésus! Je saigne aussi. Immolé le même jour . . . Mais toi, tu es mort pour quelque chose. Moi, je meurs pour rien. C'est quand même à cause de toi . . . pour toi . . . Jésus. Si tu veux . . . Et si je pouvais . . . te donner la main . . . et te voir sourire . . . Jésus . . . Mon frère . . .

Ghelderode has been such a prolific writer that it is impossible, within the scope of these few pages, to do full justice to his many-sided, tortured and uneven genius. His plays abound with misshapen buffoons, torturers, degenerate kings, lascivious monks and lecherous old men, and all these characters play out their grim charades, puppet-wise, to a kind of chorus accompaniment of ecstatic, possessed and delirious groundlings. *Hop Signor!* (1935) should be read as typical of all this. *Fastes d'Enfer* (1929), which caused a riot when it was first produced in Paris at the Marigny Theatre in 1949, shows him almost in the grip of daemonic possession as he insists on raising a giant mitred figure from the dead and transmogrifying a group of ecclesiastics into a pack of gibbering monkey-devils! *Pantagleize* (1929) was first produced in Flemish (1930) and then in French in Brussels in 1934, and is unique in having a contemporary setting: a town somewhere in Europe between one war and the next! It is a grim but hilarious extravaganza about a political revolution instigated by a grotesque group of malcontents who are led (by sheer accident) by a modern innocent, a kind of holy fool, a truly Chaplinesque character.

Ghelderode describes *Pantagleize* as 'a farce to make you sad', and into it he seems to have poured a distillation of his whole philosophical outlook. The Innocents, he tells us, are always ripe for slaughter. Dreamers and spinners of dreams, because they do no wrong other than to remain steadfast to the promptings of their instinct, are a constant danger to this de-humanized society of ours which prizes intelligence before all else and so leads to the fragmentation of all mankind. It is a gloomy philosophy but a robust one in that it does issue a challenge to mankind to come to terms with itself. Amidst a general massacre of the innocents Pantagleize can murmur:

> Je crains que cette journée n'ait été belle que pour moi. Oui, j'ai connu toutes les surprises, toutes les émotions, tous les sentiments, même celui de ma supériorité. Je suis une vedette, bien qu'ignorant tout du scénario que je joue . . .

Later he both introduces himself and excuses himself to the officer who is about to execute him:

> Je suis Pantagleize. On m'a un peu abîmé, voyez-vous!

And his dying words are a simple affirmation of the fact that he knows that he at least has truly lived:

> Quelle . . . belle . . . journée!

3

Herman CLOSSON (1901–) has always been ready to recognize the influence of Maeterlinck on his work and his indebtedness to Elizabethan playwrights in general and to Shakespeare and Marlowe in particular. He is obsessed by trickery and sees the world as one in which only traps, impostures and treachery are to be encountered. And the greatest imposture of all on a credulous public is history itself. The historians come to wrap the truth in dreams, to weave webs of myth and trickery, and in so doing hide from us for ever the true nature of the heroes on whose exploits they build in order to give to society a model of what the perfect member of that society should be. We are all haunted by the idea of grandeur. We all seek to ennoble and enrich our lives in every field of human endeavour by achieving the *grand geste*, by experiencing the supreme emotion, and we all fail because we are all pathetically human. Some few manage to strike an attitude and rise above themselves for a short spell, but they become all too quickly aware of the transient nature of this. It is the transient that the historian would have us believe is permanent. And it is the historian's treachery and his hero's real sense of insufficiency that provide the ironic and dramatic moments on which Closson builds all his plays.

That is to say, all except one. *Le Jeu des Quatre Fils Aymon* can be said to be one play in which Closson in his maturity rose above himself, struck his own attitude, abandoned his coldly lucid and critical approach, his cynicism, and set himself the task of firing the Belgians with a true sense of patriotism and spirit of resistance to overcome the dark days of German occupation during the 1940's. The play was specially written for the *Comédiens Routiers* (a kind of itinerant Rover Scout theatrical group) and it was performed in theatres and market places throughout Belgium before being finally banned by the Germans in 1941. It retells the popular legend of four brothers who, falling into displeasure with the Emperor Charlemagne, are bitterly pursued by the Emperor's armies. They take refuge with their father, Aymon, but he, as a loyal vassal, must order them to leave. They are helped by a wizard, Maugis, and also by the gift of a miraculous horse, Bayard. After many adventures in which they give proof of a rare nobility of character their generosity and prowess is finally recognized by Charlemagne. And now they are immortal and span the centuries together with Bayard, the one proof of their existence being the Bayard Rock on the banks of the Meuse near Dinant which was split in twain by the hoof of their horse as a permanent reminder to all who boldly and fearlessly resist oppression that they must (however miraculously) triumph:

> Ardenne en fleurs, Ardenne ardente,
> Pays des ciels, pays des monts,
> Pays brûlant du sang wallon,
> Ils sont vivants
> Tes Quatre fils Aymon!

Herman Closson came to prominence with the production of *Godefroid de Bouillon* (1933). In a series of fifteen tableaux (a method of presentation that Closson came to favour in that he was able to combine both dramatic intensity with continuity) he tells the whole epic story of Godefroid from his departure from Belgium on the first crusade to the capture of Jerusalem. But he tells the story in his own inimitable way. He reduces this mystical-romantic adventure of the Middle Ages to its earthly dimensions. He portrays Godefroid not as a national hero but as an ordinary mortal with all the weaknesses of the ordinary mortal. The real hero of the play is not so much Godefroid as the chronicler whose job it is to 'invent' Godefroid, to make him march in his own legend, to construct it and then justify it. Godefroid embarks on a dream crusade in a dream of the chronicler's invention to discover a dream Jerusalem. He is not a hero but an ordinary man brought face to face with heroism and he is depicted as the only man amongst all his retinue who knows himself for what he is – nothing.

In *William ou la Comédie de l'Aventure* (1938) Closson tries to show us that only the truly creative genius can resist the temptation to moments of grandeur on which the hero myth is built. It is a fantasy play set against a rich Beggar's Opera background of slums, brothels and a murderer's hide-out into which he plunges Shakespeare who has fallen in love with one, Mary, the robber's paramour. The dramatic moments of the play spring from Shakespeare's decision to sacrifice a great love for his art. And the whole story is cunningly told by fusing the play we are watching with the one Shakespeare is writing, is having rehearsed, or is himself rehearsing. Shakespeare has to choose between sacred and profane love. His choice leads to asceticism and austerity, to Shakespeare's discovery of a true faith, the theatre.

Faux-Jour (1941) is the one contemporary play Closson has given us, but he takes care to arrange an exotic jungle setting. Three colonials, living for many years far from civilization, have conceived the extraordinary idea of inviting an unknown but beautiful magazine cover girl to come and spend a holiday with them in the jungle at their expense. Even more strange, she accepts. The crude purpose of her visit is, of course, obvious. The drama centres on the reactions of the three men –Philippe the romantic idealist, Bernard the middle-aged cynic, Hubert the ageing sensualist – when their dream cover girl dissolves into flesh and blood before their eyes. Each has made his gesture, each has sought his moment of *grandeur* – and not least the girl, Lucienne, who made it by undertaking the preposterous voyage – yet none can match up to it. As Bernard somewhat poignantly puts it,

> Toute le vie, ici, est ivre de mirages. Nous promenons nos mains aveugles sur des fleurs monstrueuses. La chaleur dissout et décuple les choses. Ce n'est que par éclair, de temps à autre, que nous nous reconnaissons les uns les autres.

It would have been so simple for all of them to go to bed with Lucienne, yet none does it, nor does Lucienne encourage them to do so. All the protagonists deliberately stop the course of events and oppose them with a kind of supreme reservation. This simple refusal is something we find occurring again and again in all Closson's plays and it gives to them moments of touching dramatic intensity and pathos. We find it in *L'Epreuve du Feu* (1945), the story of a false Joan of Arc, and again in Closson's brilliant depiction of Renaissance Italy, *Borgia* (1947), when Borgia, having penetrated to Lucrèce's bedchamber, refuses to snatch a too easy victory and silently contemplates the night:

> Nous allons rester ici, tous les deux. Loin l'un de l'autre, immobiles et muets. Et prendre tout ce qui nous reste de cette nuit incomparable.

The philosophy behind all this is summed up in simple terms
for us by Bernard in *Faux-Jour*:

Il a dû vous arriver, déjà, de vous trouver devant des branches
lourdes de fruits. Et de découvrir parmi eux le plus mûr, le plus
éclatant, le plus irrésistible. Et, au moment où vous avancez la
la main, quelque chose vous force, irrésistiblement, à en prendre
un autre, un peu moins beau, un peu moins . . . *parfait*.

4

Though it was Maeterlinck who claimed that 'nous ne nous
grandissons qu'en grandissant les mystères qui nous accablent',
it was Henri SOUMAGNE (1891–1951) who, both in the theatre
and in the way in which he managed his whole life, managed also
to put this into practice. He was fascinated by man's inescapable
involvement with living; by the absurdities and paradoxes
provoked by man's humanity (and inhumanity) to man; by the
way in which the symbol often hid or distorted the truth it was
supposed to be making more accessible and needed grappling
with on its own terms if that truth was ever to be revealed. It is
in this sense that I referred earlier to Soumagne's theatre as being
the theatre of anti-symbolism, and it is also in this sense that he
owes a debt to Maeterlinck who was quick to praise his early
work as being that of a genuine scenic inventor, of the creator of
an astonishing atmosphere that betrayed a dramatic temperament of the first order.

Of strict bourgeois and Catholic upbringing, Henri Soumagne
(in private life Wagener) attended the Jesuit college of Saint
Michel in Brussels and, as he once put it to me, had to lose his
faith there 'in order to find God'. He studied law at the University of Brussels. He fought in World War I, was taken prisoner
and later interned in Switzerland (where he began writing
plays), and then came home again to embark on an immediately
successful career as a barrister which gave him full scope for
marrying his passion for social justice with an equally mounting
passion for the theatre.

In the theatre also, though his first play, *Les Epaves* (1919), was

G

not a success, he scored an immediate triumph when Lugné-Poë undertook the production of *L'Autre Messie* (1923) at the Théâtre de l'Œuvre in Paris. The reception was sensational. The play was immediately in demand in places as far apart as Berlin, Warsaw and Leningrad. And in Prague it had to be taken off because of riots it provoked from the opening night. Soumagne had had the courage to treat in theatrical terms a serious subject that was to preoccupy him all his life: that of the existence of God and of man's often incredible behaviour having once postulated this existence. Also, not only was he treating a new theme for the theatre, but he was treating it in a highly idiosyncratic way. Though detached and objective in his approach, he introduced his own peculiar whimsy and delight in paradox. He challenged the symbol to deliver up its secret by deliberate buffoonery which, by some process of alchemy, produced its own deeper spiritual level of understanding. Yet he remained a scrupulous craftsman in the best classical tradition, respecting the three unities and providing continuity for the five scenes into which the play is divided by making the actor who spoke the last lines of a preceding scene open the next one with exactly the same lines.

L'Autre Messie, reduced to its simplest dimensions, is a discussion among drunks about the existence of God. The action of the play takes place in a wretched Warsaw saloon bar with 'that characteristic smell of fried onions, sweat and intelligence that so often permeates places where Jews hang out'. The hero of the play, David Kellerstein, has become rich and is drawn by an overwhelming nostalgia to visit the scene of his earlier poverty. With the exception of a young Christian, Dmitri, all are of the Jewish faith. Kellerstein arrogantly claims that there is no God. Dmitri challenges this and offers to prove His existence to the Jew. Kellerstein chooses his weapons: the existence of God is to be decided by means of a bizarre four-round boxing bout. Kellerstein is beaten. It now remains for him to choose his own particular God. As the men get more deliriously drunk Kellerstein summons each God in turn to appear before him: Osiris, Buddha, Zeus, Jehovah and Christ. Each of them claims to have the answer to the question who is the one and true God, but Kellerstein decides that they are all impostors. Then the play builds itself up remorselessly to a most moving and dramatic end.

All the drunks remember that it is Christmas Eve. A star comes to a halt above the tavern. They are seized with the idea that God must be there, in the tavern, amongst them. Kellerstein becomes the only possible choice. After all, was his father not a carpenter? The drunks, now in a delirious frenzy, beg him to proclaim a religion, to formulate its dogmas and to give them some hope for the future. What has he to say?

> Je suis ivre, je suis Dieu. Je vous parle. Vivez, vivez, vivez . . .
> Vivez toute votre vie. Exaspérez toutes vos étreintes. Pleurez tous
> vous chants. Soyez malheureux d'une façon méticuleuse pour
> que l'un de vous peut-être ou même l'un de vos descendants,
> dans les siècles des siècles, connaisse, une minute, le bonheur
> . . . Croyez . . . Aimez . . .

> Espérez . . . Aimez tout le monde. Croyez en toute chose.
> Espérez en ce que vous voudrez. Je serai plus précis un autre soir.
> Vous l'aurez cette religion qui vous sauvera. . . .

But when? When?

> Bientôt . . . Mais aujourd'hui votre Dieu est plein comme une
> vache . . . Il ne peut cependant pas le faire, sous une table, son
> sermon sur la Montagne!

Soumagne's next play, *Bas-Noyard* (1924) was by complete contrast a gay and near-Rabelaisian farce in which he ridiculed communal elections and hinted at some of the piquant ways in which they could be rigged. A year later *Les Danseurs de Gigue*, again produced by Lugné-Poë at the Théâtre de l'Œuvre, treated in a still light-hearted way a more serious theme that pre-occupied him. Parallel lines never meet. But suppose they did? Or, to put it another way, we all of us at some time or another have the feeling that two different persons live within us; why not imagine one single individual inhabiting two separate bodies? A geometric problem, as Soumagne loved to call it, worked out with rare skill to make a most fascinating and disturbing theatrical entertainment.

Terminus (1927) was first produced in Prague and then in Paris and Brussels. Here, though still in droll and whimsical vein,

Soumagne returns to his preoccupation with death and the possibility or negation of life hereafter. Why, he asks, if we don't take life seriously, must we take death so seriously? Why does our whole attitude change when faced with death? His hero visits a fairground, enters a sideshow and is told by a Chinese magician that he will die at midnight that day. He has only a few hours to live. Friends gather around him. He is a prey to remorse and anxieties over a misspent life but much more concerned that he has to die without having left any mark at all on the world. He has intelligence which he has misused. If only during the few minutes left to him to live he could create something, leave some permanent record of his passage on earth! Midnight strikes. The minutes go by and he is still very much alive! Overboard go all his worthy resolutions. He is alive and life is to be enjoyed. The real climax comes, however, when the Chinese magician obligingly calls on him as he is in the midst of celebrating his 'release' to confess to an error in his calculations: the magician had forgotten the clocks were advanced one hour for summer time; his death will take place, therefore, at one o'clock in the morning and he has still some thirty-four minutes to live! To die a second time, so to speak, oh no, that is too much! And at that point Soumagne brings down the curtain.

Soumagne's greatest play, and the one for which quite rightly he felt the most affection, was first produced at the Théâtre de l'Œuvre in Paris in 1928. In *Madame Marie*, which he entitled a three-act mystery play, he returns again to his main preoccupation, that of the existence and meaning of God, and reconstitutes for us his interpretation of the life, passion and resurrection of Christ. Scrupulously honest as always, he treats the story with respect and near-reverence, and is paradoxically at his most poignant and moving when he is what would be termed at his most blasphemous. His careful prefatory note to the printed edition of the play betrays his intent seriousness of purpose. He says:

J'ai simplement essayé de mettre à la scène ce qui a pu se passer là-bas, voici deux mille ans bientôt. Je me suis consciencieusement documenté. Je n'ai trouvé la vérité nulle part. J'en ai déduit qu'elle a été partout. Dès lors, j'ai calmement échafaudé

une version, tout aussi exacte et tout aussi fausse que toutes celles
qui furent imaginées par les historiens, les philosophes et les
évangélistes. Il s'est fait que, dans son impiété fondamentale,
mon œuvre est toute pleine de respect mystique. Et la rencontre
fortuite de ces deux sentiments contradictoires me fut un bonheur.

Soumagne's version shows Jesus as Himself suffering deeply
with all those who suffer and possessed of the rare genius of
finding the comforting word, act and gesture to console and
uplift. As His reputation spreads so do people create His legend
and attach an importance to His work that is out of all proportion. 'They prove to me textually,' He says, 'that I am God
. . . they have loaded on My shoulders the grave responsibility
of My religion.' Simple-hearted Mary pleads with her Son to
return with her to Nazareth and has almost succeeded in getting
him to forsake the dangerous path he is treading when the arch-
villain of the play, Matthew, turns the tables and, by the sheer
force of his personality, brings the poor woman to acquiesce in
the Divinity of Christ. Matthew is in no doubt as to what is to be
made to happen. He has carefully collated the texts to prove the
Divine mission of Jesus, and, if Jesus is to be king, then he is to be
the chief minister.

In all Matthew's machinations there is a subtle and adroit
intervention on the part of Soumagne that is in no way forced, or
displeasing, but which, on the contrary, adds greatly to the
drama. Matthew not only collates the texts but he is made to
juggle with future texts in quite an arbitrary way, and also to
prophesy without knowing he is doing so. Thus, when he hears
of Christ's arrest he cites a part of Oscar Wilde's 'Ballad of
Reading Gaol' attributing the verses to 'some Roman poet
disowned by his fellow-countrymen but much admired in
Greece':

> Car chacun tue ce qu'il aime;
> L'homme brave avec une épée,
> L'homme lâche avec un sourire . . .

Matthew forces Judas to betray Christ. Judas reproaches
Matthew for his duplicity. And when Matthew hears that Judas

has hanged himself he exclaims: 'Ah! Judas, premier martyr, pardon!' Again, when Peter, a prey to doubts, asks Matthew: 'If someone said to you, "You wish to save the world but yourself you cannot save ..." ' Matthew peremptorily interrupts him:

> Ne raisonne pas! Chef de l'Eglise, sache croire, sans t'arrêter aux incohérences, ni discuter les contradictions!

At the same time Soumagne is at great pains to reveal all the nobility and greatness of purpose in the plans of Jesus and his apostles. And the climax of the play pivots on this. Once Christ is dead, Mary, who has struggled hard not to be duped by Matthew, must accept the resurrection. So must the decurion who was paid by Matthew to spirit away the dead body of Christ from the tomb. And so finally must Matthew, caught in his own toils. He thought he was inventing a God and now finds that invention cannot match up to the spiritual reality of the risen Lord:

> Je jouais ce rôle insensé. Je voulais être le Maître d'un Dieu, de sa doctrine et de son histoire. Je croyais à ma sagesse et à votre démence. La foi m'est venue, saine, bienfaisante, soudaine ... Jésus est le roi. Il est là, vivant ... Je le vois ... Il connaissait mon péché. Il devait sourire de ma démence. Jésus est vraiment un Dieu ...

All that remains for Matthew to do is to preach the Gospel he has become so involved in and await the violent and cruel death he knows lies in store. Meantime, the play closes on a note of beauty and pathos with the Virgin Mary, assured now of Her own place in the scheme of things, being invited to be the first to pray to the risen Lord. She reflects a moment, and then:

> Je sais un cantique qu'il aimait. Il m'en a appris les préceptes salutaires. Il m'a formé à la divine leçon. Bien qu'adressée à Jahweh, c'est pour la gloire de Jésus que nous oserons murmurer cette prière: 'Père nôtre qui êtes aux cieux ...'

Apart from *Le Buste de Cire* (1931), *S.S. Baltimore* (1932), *L'Arbre de la Liberté* (1945), which he wrote in collaboration with

Georges Sion to celebrate the liberation of Belgium after World War II, and an adaptation of Goethe's *Egmont* (1945) – plays which he dismissed lightly as *trivia* – Soumagne found nothing more to say in the theatre. Instead, he turned his attention more and more to the law courts, and from his researches he gave us three fascinating reconstructions of past crimes in which he probed with sure dramatic instinct not only into the psychological motivation behind the crimes but also into the effect the criminal drama had on the populace at large. *L'Etrange Monsieur Courtois* (1943) recaptured the curious story of a police inspector who was also the leader of a gang of thieves and most probably an assassin as well. *Chiennes d'Enfer* (1944) told how a promising barrister and politician came to kill his actress wife. And *Le Seigneur de Bury* (1946), easily the best (and the one on which I was privileged to see him lavish so much care and attention as regards style and atmosphere), tells how a dissolute aristocrat came to kill his brother-in-law with nicotine poisoning in order to inherit his estate.

5

Two playwrights who came to prominence at the end of World War II are Suzanne LILAR (1901–   ) and Georges SION (1913–   ). Madame Lilar was born in Ghent and her husband is a member of the Antwerp bar and has been several times Minister of Justice since the last war. Françoise Mallet-Joris, their talented daughter, has already established herself as a novelist of considerable promise.

Madame Lilar had an immediate success with the production of *Le Burlador* at the Théâtre Saint-Georges in Paris in 1947. Though she treated a threadbare theme – that of Don Juan, the seducer – she tackled it from a novel and unusually feminine angle. If her Don Juan calls himself *le burlador* (the betrayer) she goes on to show that it is himself whom he is deceiving. He is profoundly human, though he might wish it otherwise. And there is purity in him despite his vaunted sexual appetites. If he takes so many women to himself it is because he does fall in love with them, and he becomes lost in a labyrinth of his own contrivance,

lost among the many faces of love. In consequence it is he who
suffers. He has to identify himself with his victims and every
cruelty he inflicts carries with it its own punishment. He is
consumed in his own fire.

The same theme is taken up again in a different guise in *Tous
les Chemins Mènent au Ciel* (1947) which has its setting in a *béguinage* in Ghent during the fourteenth century. As Madame
Lilar herself puts it in explanation of the play, which has been
described as a kind of theological drama:

> Les femmes sont prêtes toujours à vouer leurs attendrissements
> à ce qui se présente. Et si ce n'est à l'homme, c'est à Dieu. Le
> tout avec une pareille aisance.

Like *le burlador*, the nun heroine of this play is in quest of the
absolute, and like him she must weave her way through the dark
labyrinth of her own heart, through stages of exalted sensualism
rivalling with mystical yearning, until, ravaged by the struggle,
she finds a rare peace and a sublime quietude of mind.

George Sion's first play, *La Matrone d'Ephèse* (1942), based on a
tale from Petronius (compare Christopher Fry's *A Phoenix too
Frequent*), immediately captivated by its bubbling sense of
humour, its warmth, freshness and spontaneity. With *Charles le
Téméraire* (1944) Sion, in more ambitious vein, chronicled the
struggles and ambitions of Charles the Bold and adroitly related
them to the history of that part of the Lowlands today known as
Belgium. The time-span of the play is from 1461, before Charles
inherits the title of Duke of Burgundy, to 1477 when he is killed
in battle before Nancy. The poetry, pathos, nobility and
generosity of mind that lay behind all the mixed feelings of the
various protagonists of this turbulent period in history is skilfully
exposed and interwoven to heighten the drama of each situation,
and the whole story is told with satisfying classical restraint and
a sense of completeness. Thus, as his father lies dying in Bruges,
Charles is moved by the beauty of the scene and the awful
responsibility of the moment:

> Il fait beau dans Bruges aujourd'hui. C'est dimanche, et le mois
> de juin. Si vous pouviez voir le ciel . . . Il est doux comme un
> satin. Et l'on devine, plus beau encore, au loin, le ciel qui est sur

la mer. Le soir va bientôt descendre avec ses cloches, et l'on chantera complies dans les églises . . . Je garderai tout ce que vous me laissez, nos terres de Flandres et leurs vieilles tapisseries, Brabant le nourricier, Namur et Luxembourg avec leurs forêts, Liège qui est aussi belle que Rome sur la rivière de Meuse, le duché de Bourgogne, dont vous aimiez les vins, Dijon, où nous sommes nés . . . Vous me verrez de loin administrant notre bien, rendant la justice qui est la vertu reine.

All Charles's ambitions to rule over a territory that will extend from Bruges to Italy are frustrated and when he dies in battle he leaves his daughter in a most perilous position. He appears to her in a vision she has at her palace in Ghent and prophetically excuses himself:

Songe aux pays que je te laisse. Ils sont beaux comme tous les pays d'entre-deux. Ils doivent faire leur chemin entre de grands Etats, comme entre des montagnes, difficilement . . . Ils ont besoin de paix, et ils servent la paix. Etait-ce un rêve, nos terres de Bruges à l'Italie? On en eût fait un immense fleuve de richesse et de travail, un fleuve qui traversait l'Europe . . . A son départ, la terre belge, péniche amarrée au nord, pesante comme une île et chargée d'opulence . . . N'oublie jamais ton destin. Je te laisse de grands pays qui ont une grande mission. J'ai essayé de l'accomplir. J'y ai succombé . . . Prie encore . . . Adieu . . .

With *La Princesse de Chine* (1951), Sion returned to the whimsical style of *La Matrone d'Ephèse* to dramatize a fable of Turandot. *Le Voyageur de Foreceloup* (1951) is a deliberately prosaic and serious attempt at showing what depths of suffering must be plumbed if genuine disinterested goodness is to prevail. Not only can Sion's mysterious traveller take unto himself with God's grace the physical suffering of others (as does Violaine in Claudel's *L'Annonce Faite à Marie*), but he can even be brought to lose his faith so that others may regain theirs. *La Malle de Pamela* (1955) is another light and frothy exercise that gives enormous theatrical pleasure. Since when, apart from some extremely competent translations from Shakespeare, executed on commission for various theatrical managements, Sion has remained silent. And this is a pity.

6

Among what may be loosely termed the modern generation of Belgian dramatists writing in French three names predominate. These are José André LACOUR (1919–   ), Charles BERTIN (1919–   ) and Jean MOGIN (1921–   ). Lacour's first play, *Tristan* (1943), was quickly followed by several other experimental efforts that won him increasing recognition but no firm standing. Then, in 1958, came *L'Année du Bac* which created an immediate sensation on its opening night in Paris at the Théâtre Edouard VII. Never before has a playwright attempted (and with such conspicuous success) to catch the modern idiom of the post-war generation of adolescents, groping their way to manhood and womanhood, pathetically vulnerable, pathetically loyal, brittle yet resilient:

'C'est terrible de ne plus croire en son père, Maman. On . . . on devient si vieux tout d'un coup. . . .

Quel bon Dieu de droit avons-nous de tant exiger d'eux, Mic? C'est parce qu'ils sont 'notre papa' que ça les oblige à être des héros, des saints ou des génies? Pourquoi ne pas les laisser tranquilles, nos vieux? Et pourquoi se flanquer une balle dans la tête chaque fois qu'ils n'ont pas été à la hauteur?

Charles Bertin started his dramatic career with *Les Prétendants* (1947) which was later performed in English at the Birmingham Repertory Theatre (1950) with the title *Love in a Labyrinth*. It is a modern version of the story of Ulysses: man returning from the last war and endeavouring to reconstruct his lost inner life in a world that has ceased to know the meaning of such a life. With *Don Juan* (1948) Bertin gives us a debauchee who sins in the imagination rather than in the flesh and whose tragedy is that he can never know the fulfilment of love shared. *Les Folies Bergère* (1950) returns to the middle-class provincial setting of his first work and shows us three people (mother, father and son) passionately yet antagonistically attached to one another. *Christophe Colomb* was specially re-written from a radio play (which won Bertin the *Prix Italia* prize in 1953) and first performed at the Brussels World Exhibition in 1958.

With this play Bertin proved his unerring skill as a dramatist who can use his remarkable poetic gifts in the theatre both to create atmosphere and also to build up a scene and achieve high moments of dramatic intensity. The action takes place on board the *Santa Maria*, either in Columbus's cabin (where the dramatic moments of the play are worked out) or on the bridge among the crew, which becomes the centre of the poetic action of the play. Thus, the deck scenes, alternating with those in the cabin, form a kind of counterpoint to the main action which is concerned with the various temptations Columbus must meet and overcome if he is to fulfil his mission and his destiny. These temptations are of three kinds: material, in that the crew is concerned with its own personal safety; spiritual, in that the ship's chaplain opposes to Columbus's design the arguments and authority of the Church; sentimental, in that Alonzo, the second in command of the expedition and the close friend of Columbus, is won over by the chaplain to betray his master. Columbus triumphs, but in his triumph he finds himself supremely alone if supremely sure of himself. If he has at last found land, however, he has also found himself, and his pride consists less in having done what he set out to do than in having proved his own soul. Thus at the final curtain Columbus is discovered on his knees before the Crucifix, his arms spread out in adoration, and the noise of the sea is suddenly drowned by a swelling chorus of sailors' voices jubilantly singing the *Gloria in Excelsis Deo* he has ordered.

Jean Mogin achieved immediate success with his first play, *A Chacun Selon Sa Faim*, which was produced at the Théâtre du Vieux-Colombier in Paris in 1950 and won him the Lugné-Poë prize as the best play of the year. It is a play of great austerity, vigorously written yet with an economy of words that serves to heighten the dramatic intensity and portray most vividly the violent clash of character on which the plot turns. Significantly the setting is a Spanish nunnery, but the harsh and burning intolerance of Spanish faith is subtly combined with a Flemish mystical and Jansenist approach. The abbess, Maria de Mello, will suffer no intermediary between God and herself, and becomes in consequence a soul that is crazed because it yearns for the absolute. She revolts against the Vicar-General less from pride than because her longing for God is greater than her pride, and all that comes between God and herself distracts her from God. Her error springs from a monstrous need for purity and it is this that determines the tragic sequence of events which follows.

The other major play of Jean Mogin (who is at present in charge of drama production with the Belgian broadcasting system) is *La Fille à la Fontaine*, which was first produced at a dramatic festival at Nîmes in July 1955 and then by the Belgian National Theatre in October 1956. Mogin again returns to the theme of a quest for absolute purity, but he now confines it to the impossible situation in which two Italian peasant lovers find themselves because they will not and cannot conform with what is generally expected of them in their bawdy peasant surroundings:

> Cela me fait peur de vivre comme les autres, d'échouer comme les autres, de renoncer comme eux. Tous ces faux couples sur le parvis des églises m'effraient. Ces filles en blanc, je les vois enveloppées d'un suaire et déjà prêtes à l'enterrement de leur amour. Cette nuit de consécration qui les attend, veillée par les amis goguenards et les cousins libidineux, pour moi, c'est une veillée funèbre.

The firm resolve of Ruggero leads first of all to an incomprehension on the part of Chiari which matches the puzzlement of the villagers, but finally Chiari is won over. 'Ours is the quintessence of pure love,' she says, to which the priest replies (speaking for the villagers, whether he knows it or not):

> Vous êtes le refus, refus de vivre, refus de se soumettre à l'ordinaire condition. Vous avez refusé le monde, et puis vous vous êtes refusés entre vous; enfin le monde vous a repoussés. Maintenant vous êtes solitaires et divisés.

'No,' retorts Chiari, 'we are united as never before, and unsullied.' But the trial has proved too much for her. As she finally falls into the arms of Ruggero she is a dying woman and it is a corpse that he carries to the nuptial chamber, though he cannot and will not accept the fact:

Elle entre dans sa maison de jeune femme. Elle va se réveiller dans sa chambre de noces. Mais il faut qu'elle dorme d'abord; et je vais enfermer les coqs trop matinaux; je vais jeter de la paille sur le trottoir, sous sa fenêtre; *je vais boucher, dans le volet, ce jour en forme de cœur que la lumière traverse!* Je vous dis qu'elle dort! Je m'allongerai contre elle et j'attendrai qu'elle rouvre les yeux. Je vous dis qu'elle dort!

It is a curiously disturbing play, severe and without concessions of any kind, and shot through with symbolism of the kind I have placed in italics in the above extract from the final poignant speech of Ruggero. It is also, in another sense, a play about lack of communication and as such has its disturbing message for the times. It is a play that begins where Maeterlinck left off, for Maeterlinck's attitude, ultimately, is that the external world is not important. Mogin gives the lie to this. If you deny the very real existence of that external world you do so at your own peril. Mogin also provides a counterblast to Crommelynck who delighted (as I said earlier) in depicting characters carried away by the folly of being. Mogin's characters are destroyed because of their refusal to 'be'. From all these points of view Mogin is one of the most promising dramatists of the present age, the one most truly Belgian in the sense I have tried to convey this in the introductory section of Chapter Nine.

Select Bibliography

DE BACKER, F.   *Contemporary Flemish Literature*, Brussels, 1924
BITHELL, J.   *Contemporary Belgian Poetry*, London, 1911
Life and Writings of Maeterlinck, London, 1913
Contemporary Belgian Literature, London, 1915
Contemporary Flemish Poetry, London, 1917
CAMMAERTS, E.   *The Treasure House of Belgium*, London, 1924
CHARLIER, G.   *Les lettres françaises en Belgique*, Brussels, 1938
CLOSSET, F.   *Aspects et figures de la littérature flamande*, Brussels, 1944
HALLS, W. D.   *Maurice Maeterlinck*, London, 1960
HAMÉLIUS, P.   *La littérature française et flamande de Belgique*, Brussels, 1921
HANLET, C.   *Les écrivains belges contemporains*, 2 vols., Liège, 1946
MATHEWS, A. J.   *La Wallonie, The Symbolist Movement in Belgium*, New York, 1947
DE RIDDER, A.   *La littérature flamande contemporaine*, Paris, 1923
WEEVERS, T.   *Poetry of the Netherlands in its European Context*, London, 1960
WILMOTTE, M.   *La culture française en Belgique*, Paris, 1911

Index